REKINDLE THE SPARK

10 STEPS TO REVITALISE YOUR RELATIONSHIP

Barbara Duff

www.relationshipsandlove.org

ORPEN PRESS

158.2

Published by
Orpen Press
Upper Floor, Unit K9
Greenogue Business Park
Rathcoole
Co. Dublin
Ireland
email: info@orpenpress.com
www.orpenpress.com

© Barbara Duff, 2017

Paperback ISBN 978-1-78605-038-0
ePub ISBN 978-1-78605-039-7

Printed in Dublin by SPRINTprint Ltd

To Desmond, who has taught me the true meaning of love

ABOUT THE AUTHOR

Barbara Duff has been working as a marriage counsellor for the past twenty-six years. She is an accredited member of the National Association for Pastoral Counselling and Psychotherapy (NAPCP) and author of *The Ten Secrets to a Happy and Long-Lasting Relationship*.

Barbara is an expert in the field of psychosexual and relationship counselling. Her work is dedicated to all couples who are experiencing difficulties in their relationship, helping them recognise whatever problems they may have, and equipping them with the skills to tackle the issues themselves. She sees the role of counselor/therapist not as someone in control, but as a facilitator.

Barbara's work is influenced by many of the current therapy models, but mostly by the cognitive behavioural and systemic therapy approaches. She is also informed by her thirty years as an educator.

Barbara blogs about new trends and developments in the field of psychotherapy at www.relationshipsandlove.org.

She has recently launched her flagship product – Rekindle the Spark: Save Your Marriage – an innovative online self-help programme for couples, on which this book is based.

Barbara is happily married and lives in Dublin. She has four children and eleven grandchildren.

Acknowledgements

Firstly, I wish to thank all the couples with whom I have worked over the past twenty-seven years. Your courage, strength and dignity are my inspiration. As we journeyed together through the labyrinths and intricacies of human relationships, you have managed to keep faith in one another and most importantly in yourselves.

Next, I want to acknowledge the role of my erstwhile colleagues and students in secondary education. My almost thirty years as a teacher in St Andrew's College, Dublin has given me invaluable insight into human relationships and the learning process. My students have taught me that the first challenge in teaching is to realise that everyone sees things from a slightly different viewpoint. The second challenge is to remove fear of the unknown.

To my colleagues in Accord, Relate and NAPCP my thanks for being always open to new ideas and approaches. Your professionalism and commitment have enhanced my continued development as a therapist.

I wish to thank especially my supervisor, Marie Daly, whose ability to see things from another perspective has provoked me to strive constantly for greater understanding of the human condition.

Thanks to the team in Orpen Press and especially to my editor, Eileen O'Brien, whose meticulous care and helpful suggestions are much appreciated.

I feel blessed to get so much happiness out of life both as teacher and therapist. But my greatest source of joy and inspiration comes from my family, our four children, Sheila, Michael, Claire and Rebecca, and my beloved husband, Desmond, who is my rock and my strength.

TABLE OF CONTENTS

WELCOME TO *REKINDLE THE SPARK*

Welcome to *Rekindle the Spark*, the ten-step programme designed to help you create and maintain a happy and lasting relationship. In ten practical steps you will learn how to transform a humdrum or even unhappy relationship into something that is exciting, caring and meaningful.

This programme is designed for couples who want to improve their relationship. It will help you reflect on your marriage to date and in particular to look at ways to enhance the quality of your communication – the keystone to a healthy relationship.

Every aspect of our lives benefits from reflection. We have check-ups for our health, our finances, even our cars. Yet somehow, few of us take time to reflect on our relationship with the most important person in our lives. So this is your chance.

Working as a counsellor gives an insight into the interaction in couple relationships – the simple things that can go wrong at times – and then the small steps that can be taken to bring about positive change. Indeed I consider it a privilege to do this work.

When we get married we embark on a lifelong journey together. We are armed with love for each other and lots of hope. But it is good from time to time to take a look at some of the behaviour patterns that have developed and see if we could learn a few extra skills. And that is what you will find in this book. We look at the art of good listening, how we express feelings and how to resolve differences in a loving way.

So who could benefit from following this programme? Whether you have been married for seven years or, like me, for 47 years, there is a lot to be gained from focusing on the two of you as a couple – to see what is so good about being together but also to realise that all couples have challenges to face.

For example, once children come along, as every parent knows, our focus shifts and rightly so. But with that shift in focus, there is a risk of losing sight of the couple you once were. Yet I am convinced that children thrive best not just by receiving love from their parents, but by witnessing their parents' love for one another.

Remember the good old days when you and your partner were getting to know each other? Remember that spark? Well, you can experience those feelings once again. The key to a happier relationship lies right here ready to be discovered by you.

Each step in this programme addresses a particular area of your relationship. Each step presents you with tasks. Some of these tasks are written assignments; others require specific action by you.

To complete all of the tasks requires dedicated *time* and *effort* from you. But don't worry – it will not take too much time. In fact, many couples have found that they enjoy the exercises so much that they happily spend more and more time on them as the programme progresses.

Each practical exercise will give you some insight into your relationship. There are just two requirements to do this effectively – a notebook or computer and dedicated time. The computer works fine but some people like to treat themselves to a notebook specifically for the written exercises, and keep it for future reference.

As for time, that depends on you but the minimum time suggested is one hour per session. So be kind to yourselves – give your relationship the attention it deserves. You will soon feel the benefit.

Some couples aim to complete a step per week, so the programme would take ten weeks in all. But be guided by what works best for you.

If your partner is unwilling or unable to participate in the programme, don't worry. By following the course and doing the exercises, you will start a shift in the dynamic between you. I call this the power of one. Your change in attitude and behaviour will impress your spouse and most likely arouse their curiosity. So don't be surprised if they opt in after all.

Welcome to *Rekindle the Spark*

If at any stage you have difficulty with the programme, visit the trouble-shooting guide at www.relationshipsandlove.org.

Best wishes,
Barbara Duff
September 2017

Step One

KNOWING MYSELF – WHO AM I?

Many people have difficulty in answering the above question. Sure, we can all list our name, age, address and occupation. But naming what makes you *you* – naming your values, needs, ambitions and expectations – can be quite a challenge. Yet, until you know yourself, the chances of getting to know another person intimately are slim. Hence this first and vital step of the programme.

How Well Do You Know Yourself?

Step One starts by tracing the various factors that have contributed to forming and moulding the person you are today. You will be guided on your journey by the questions in the assignments. We will then look at your needs as a person and a partner.

Your Picture or Idea of Yourself

Let's look at how your self-image was formed. As a child you saw yourself as reflected by others. If you were lucky enough to be surrounded by a loving and supportive family, you felt secure and saw yourself as lovable. If, on the other hand, you were raised in a difficult family situation, you may have felt insecure and lacking in self-confidence. In other words, perhaps you were not sure that you were lovable. Do you consider yourself lovable now?

But even if you came from a loving family, when you ventured into the world outside of home you saw another reflection of yourself in the eyes of others. Perhaps you were not perceived as a warm and lovable person, but were seen at times as weak or not likeable. Were you seen as a threat to the popularity of others? In that case you may have been bullied. Being the victim of bullying can leave you feeling vulnerable and insecure.

Maybe when you mixed with peers you became aggressive because you saw that behaviour as the best form of defence. Indeed, you may still behave in this way. You then became the bully, ready to sacrifice the happiness of others so that you could keep your place at the centre of attention.

Whatever happened in your childhood, you developed a role for yourself in relation to other people – the friend, the carer, the people-pleaser, the victim, the clown, the bully, to name but a few. And that role has reinforced your self-image.

You as a Young Adult

By the time you were a young adult, you had probably formed a more definite picture of yourself. You may also have become aware that you could show different facets or sides of yourself in different situations. You were experimenting with the person you thought you were and the person you wanted to become. Can you remember some of the roles you played? If you had romantic relationships in your teens they probably tended to be short-lived as you yourself continued to change and develop.

You Today

All this is a natural part of growing up. But now that you have embarked on a long-term relationship you need to be quite secure and happy with the person you are today. You are the product of all the experiences, both positive and negative, that you have had since you were born. You need to get to know and accept the child, adolescent and adult that make the person you are. Now that you have grown and developed, it is time to decide on the things that matter most to you in life. Once you have identified what is really important to you, you will be able to look for matching qualities and values in your partner.

So your task in Step One is to get to know yourself. Give yourself the time you deserve. I hope that you will enjoy this journey of self-discovery.

Get your notebook and pen or sit at your computer for your first session. Make sure that you are in a quiet place, free from distractions. Remember, the more open and honest you are with yourself, the more you will get from the programme.

SESSION ONE

Now for the most important person in your world – YOURSELF. There are 25 questions below. But don't worry, some of them can be answered with just a word or two. Others require a little more time. The good news is that they will help you on your journey of self-discovery.

Introduction

1. Start by what you know – name, age, address. Next write about 'Me as I see myself'. Try to capture the essential you, listing your qualities and personality.
2. What does it feel like to be you? Are you generally happy with the person you are? Write your response.

Your Past

Next is your story. Here you explore some of the factors that have contributed to making you the person you are today. Look at your position in your family, how you bonded with the significant people in your early life and how you coped with challenging experiences. This helps paint a picture of you as a younger person.

3. Where do you come from – location, environment?
4. What were your family values as you grew up? Try naming at least three. Or, can you name three important messages or family rules as you grew up?
5. How did you relate to your mother?
6. How did you relate to your father?
7. Where are you positioned in your family?
8. How did you get along with your siblings as you grew up?
9. Can you recall feeling proud of yourself as a child? Describe the event.
10. Who was the most important person to you when you were growing up?
11. Did you experience loss as a child – loss of a parent, a friend, falling out of favour?
12. If so, how did you deal with the loss?
13. Were there things or people you were afraid of as a child?
14. Did you tell anyone about your fears?
15. Can you recall being praised? By whom?
16. Did you receive physical affection as a child? From whom?
17. Did you feel loved as a child?

Read over what you have written. Think of the child you were. How did that child feel? Now that you are an adult, what would you like to say to that child? Can you look lovingly on your younger self? Can you accept that child and say, 'It's all ok'? Can you allow yourself to feel proud of how you dealt with any negative experiences?

SESSION TWO

Your Present

In this session the task is to reflect on the person you are today. Continue writing the answers in your notebook.

18. You are the product of all your life's experiences, of what happened to you when you were three and thirteen and twenty-three. What challenging experiences stand out for you now as you look back? Write about two of them.
19. How did these experiences shape the person you are today? What messages did you take from them?
20. How easily do you express your emotions?
21. What triggers anger for you?
22. How do you express your anger?
23. What are your greatest fears today?
24. What are your priorities now? Name the three most important things in life for you today.
25. Do you like the person you see when you look at yourself in the mirror? Write about it.

Take as long as you need for this exercise. It may take a few sessions to complete. But that is fine. The important thing is that you get time to think about yourself.

N.B. Some childhood memories can be too difficult to handle alone. If you have experienced abuse as a child, you should seek professional counselling for this.

Pause for Thought – Who Can Make Me Happy?

Now that you have traced an outline of your developing self, what are your thoughts? Do you wish that you had received more love, more encouragement as a child? Or do you feel that your parents did the best they could to nurture and love you? Whatever your experiences of love and attachment have been, it is important that you now take responsibility for your own sense of self, for your own happiness.

The truth is that no one can make anyone else truly happy. Yes, we all love to be loved, to feel valued and appreciated and special. But no matter how much others – parents, friends or family – try, they cannot force us to be happy. Ultimately, we must realise that true happiness comes from within ourselves.

Remember your teenage years? Did you feel under pressure to conform to the fashions or trends of the day? Did you think that you had to look 'perfect' by someone else's standards before you could venture out into the social scene?

It is easy to lose your identity in a mass culture. And youth culture can be very pervasive – wherever you look you are bombarded by images of the prevailing idea of the ideal.

Maybe you struggled somewhat during those teenage years as you formulated a sense of an authentic you. Most young people do – adolescence is a time of exploration and experimentation. When you look back at your adolescent self, do you think you made good choices?

Accepting the Past

If you are unhappy with some of the choices you made when you were younger, think about that. What are your dominant feelings – regret, guilt, self-blame, blaming others? Now try to forgive your younger self and others and then move on. For if you still harbour guilt and regret from the past, you are unlikely to be happy with yourself today.

Forgiveness means letting go. Can you let go? If you find that difficult to do, try to imagine how that would be. You would be freed from the burden of negative thoughts. Think of how light you would feel – having escaped from the stress of negativity that weighs you down. Once you can imagine that stress-free state, you will find it easier to allow yourself the luxury of forgiveness.

And don't forget that the past has passed. You can no longer control it. So let it go.

SESSION THREE

Part A: The Perceptions of Others – How You See Yourself Reflected by Other People

1. On a new page write about yourself as you think others see you. Think of the feedback you get from friends, family or colleagues. What impressions do other people have of you?
2. How do you want others to think of you? Write down a few qualities.
3. Read over both accounts of you. Are there differences? Which version of you do you like best?

Part B: Looking to the Future

By now I hope that you feel more familiar with the person you are. Have you been able to address any areas of yourself that make you uncomfortable? Remember, no matter what experiences you have had in the past, you are now an adult and are responsible for yourself. And only you can change you.

You have six assignments in this section. Write as much as you can on each topic. Avoid doing them all at the same sitting – it is best to focus on one or two at a time.

1. My ambitions for myself
2. What I admire most in others
3. What I would most like to change in myself
4. How I can make that change happen
5. Things that make me happy
6. My ambitions for my relationship with my partner

Feedback

You have now completed the written assignments for Stage One. Read over your notes. I hope that you feel proud of yourself for being honest and open. Your journey of self-discovery has begun. All you have to do now is keep working on small changes that will make you feel happier in yourself. This in turn will have a positive knock-on effect on your relationship with your partner.

Stay positive. Look at how much you contribute to this relationship. Be more aware of all your good qualities. Be kind to yourself – that way you will look more kindly on your partner. Let go of chronic regret or disappointment.

If you are still unhappy, try to work out how much you can do to help yourself without relying on others to do this for you. Remember that happiness comes from within. That is why it is important to start by assessing yourself.

ONGOING EXERCISE

Self-Focus Exercise

When did you last take a good look at yourself? Have you a full-length mirror in your bathroom or bedroom? If not, install one. When drying yourself after a shower or bath, look at yourself in the mirror. Get to know your body. Accept it. Feel comfortable with it. Your body is as much a part of you as your mind is. Get used to looking at yourself.

If you are unhappy about your body, take another look. Maybe you would like to be slimmer or heavier. Fine, but that is for the future. Today, you need to accept your body as it is right now. Why let your life slip by while waiting for the magic moment when you feel totally satisfied with your body?

Avoid the pitfall of perfectionism. Some people set standards of perfection for themselves that are impossible to achieve. They therefore doom themselves to constant failure. Result? They give up and continue the cycle of unhappiness within themselves. This is a real shame as it prevents them from making positive changes.

So start living with yourself today. Accept that person in the mirror; be happy with what you have. Choose three good aspects of your body. It may be your strong muscular legs, your height, your hips, your smile or your sensuous shape. Keep looking at yourself until you find the features you are happiest with. You are not allowed to claim there are none.

Make this exercise part of your daily routine. Don't worry if you feel awkward about doing it at first. That just indicates that you have got a bit out of touch with your body. Now is the time to get back in touch. Remember, it is only when you have accepted yourself and feel comfortable with yourself that you can fully accept and love another person.

YOU HAVE NOW COMPLETED STEP ONE – WELL DONE!

PLEASE NOTE: Some things can be too big to handle on your own. If an issue arises at any stage of this programme which seems too much for you to deal with, e.g. if you were abused as a child, or if you are in an abusive relationship, please seek professional help.

Step Two

KNOWING MY PARTNER – WHO ARE YOU?

For this step, the focus is on your insight into the next most important person in your life – your spouse and partner. To love someone deeply requires a deep knowledge of that person.

It is perhaps strange but true that after months and even years together, your partner may remain a mystery in some respects. Perhaps you have been so preoccupied with the day-to-day busyness of life that you have not had time to notice. But one day you may look at your partner across the table and think – do I really know this person?

Step Two addresses your knowledge of your partner and the nature of your relationship. The assignments here will help you to assess how well you know the person with whom you share your life so intimately. You will also come to realise that getting to know your partner is a work in progress. None of us stays static – that is why it is important to keep up to date with each other as you journey through life together.

Love on the Brain

Every heart sings a song, incomplete, until another heart whispers back – Plato, c.428–348 BC

Why do we look for a loving partner with whom to share our lives? What is this love that binds us together? It is a survival imperative. As Dr Sue Johnson says in *Hold Me Tight*, we humans are caught up in emotions that are part of a survival programme set out by millions of years of evolution. We are hardwired to seek and need love. From the moment of birth, babies need love so they can develop and thrive. The need for love is as important as the need for nourishment and shelter.

This need is still there when we are adults. The special emotional bond called love attaches us to one another. We seek a life partner who makes us feel secure, who will give us the emotional protection we need to survive the challenges and trials of life. Neuroscientists have now established that the brain codes the touch and emotional response of a loved one as safety. We secrete the hormone oxytocin when we connect in a loving way with another.

Conversely, when we feel rejected or excluded by a loved one we feel hurt. Naomi Eisenberger of the University of California has conducted brain-imaging studies showing that rejection or exclusion triggers the same circuits in the same part of the brain, the anterior cingulate, as physical pain. No wonder then that we talk of 'feeling hurt' or of being 'heartbroken'.

Feeling Safe

When you enjoy a safe attachment with your partner, you feel valued and free to be yourself. There is no pressure to conform or indeed perform. You feel that you are appreciated and loved for being your true self.

Psychologist John Bowlby was the first to formulate this theory of attachment. He maintains that lovers are connected by what he calls a 'neural net'. When tuned in emotionally, lovers can help each other reach a physical and emotional balance that promotes optimal functioning.

Conversely, if there is an imbalance in the relationship – if one partner is constantly in control – the other partner may feel uneasy, unsafe or insecure. Keeping the peace becomes all-important. There can be an atmosphere of fear and/or intimidation, a sense of walking on eggshells when these couples are together. This type of relationship is unhealthy – it is based on what John Bowlby describes as an unsafe attachment.

Relationship Stages – Where Is Your Seesaw?

The best image I have found to represent a couple relationship is the seesaw. Remember being on a seesaw when you were a child? The key to making it fun was to have a partner whose weight more or less balanced your own. That way, each of you was able to be on top and then swing down to allow the other go up. So too with couples – there needs to be a fair balance of power so that no one is habitually on top or bottom.

So how did you two end up on the same seesaw? There are many theories and philosophies on the nature and development of the couple relationship. But the overall consensus is that most couples go through certain stages as their relationship matures and develops. I have outlined some of these phases here. They are not necessarily in chronological order – after many years of marriage you may find that there are still new challenges to face. That is perfectly normal. The important question is how you react when these challenges occur.

1. *In love or infatuated?* Remember the euphoric sensation you felt when you first experienced a strong attraction to your partner? This phase even has its own register of language. Did you *fall in love;* were you *swept off your feet;* or were you *bowled over* or even *blown away*? What do you notice about these phrases? They are all events or actions that happened to you – they imply that you were somehow taken over by an outside force. You did nothing, you were simply passive – almost a victim.

   Yet the great adrenalin rush of this first stage can be very exciting. The thrill of seeing your beloved, of hearing that special voice, of feeling the magic touch of that hand create deep impressions that are lodged in your memory bank.

   Some people even become addicted to being infatuated. You know those serial relationship people? They tend to fall in love over and over again. Then as soon as a relationship meets with the challenges of a deeper love they jump ship. But as you have already discovered, if a relationship is to last it must progress to something deeper in which both of you are active, not passive, participants.

Not all people experience infatuation. For some couples, their love grows and develops in a more gradual way. Perhaps they have known each other for quite a while before romance blossoms.

2. *Power adjustment*: This comes after the initial euphoria, when you realise that building a meaningful relationship requires adjustment from both of you. You know you have arrived at this stage when you have your first row or difference of opinion. Who decides where to go, what to do? Which of you compromises? What will happen next time?

   Each partner struggles to maintain harmony in the relationship without sacrificing their own autonomy and independence. This is often when break-ups occur – one partner feels that the cost of staying in the relationship is just too high.

3. *Mutual respect*: To have survived the challenges of the power struggle means that you have both developed a new and deeper respect for one another. Romance has now matured and stabilised. The seesaw keeps moving – there will always be differences of opinion, there will always be times when you have to compromise. But the key factor now is that you can love more consciously. You each recognise that your partner is the person most qualified to help you grow, to become your best self.

4. *Acceptance*: When you reach this stage the overall reaction or feeling is one of relief. You know that you are fully accepted as the person you are. Arguments are fewer and when they occur they are resolved more easily and in a respectful way. There are no more mind games; you have learned to be honest and open with one another.

5. *Equilibrium*: Now at last you have become a true couple – you realise that you are on the same team. When

challenges occur you face them together. You are not competing for power or control – you are happy to share the seesaw ride with a partner who balances you so well.

When the Unexpected Occurs

No matter how well you think you know each other, there may be times when your partner's attitude or behaviour takes you by surprise. If this happens, try to look on it as a positive. It is just an illustration of the beauty and the challenge of relationships – there is always something new to be discovered about the other person, just as there is always more to be discovered about the self – some hidden talent, depth of feeling, unrealised ambition.

Life involves change. You are constantly growing and developing as an individual. So is your spouse. The person you married and with whom you are sharing your life is not the same today as when you first started your life together. So the challenge of knowing your partner never ends.

What are your partner's ambitions? You are not sure? Time to find out. Remember that without an intimate knowledge of one another, your relationship is at risk. If there are too many gaps in your knowledge of each other, there can be too many possibilities of revelations in the future that you may find disturbing. You need to feel comfortable with this person with whom you are sharing your life.

When Trust Issues Arise

Trust and respect are essential building blocks in a relationship. Building trust requires time and patience. Like respect, trust is something that has to be earned. You must convince your partner that you are reliable and respectful of them. Because when you trust someone you feel confident that they respect and appreciate you. You believe in that person.

When **trust issues** arise, there is a shift in the dynamic of the relationship. Sometimes one partner feels insecure and worries about being deceived. What happens then? You may resort to prying into text messages, emails and other areas of your partner's private life. This snooping can only be destructive.

If you are worried about what your spouse is up to, address the issue. Talk it out. Don't make an accusation but ask for an explanation for what is worrying you. Tell your partner that you do not want to break the trust between you, but you need to feel confident that you are getting a truthful answer.

How does a situation of lack of trust come about in the first place? All too easily is the answer. If a couple does not allocate regular, dedicated time to just themselves the relationship can easily slip into a dull place. Perhaps you have been drifting along quite happily without really noticing your partner; you have not been focusing on the relationship, trusting that all is well. But has a gulf between you and your partner developed? A gulf that has been slowly widening? So it is good that you are now doing this relationship check-up.

If there is a breakdown of trust in a relationship, the whole structure of the relationship can be undermined. The cornerstone has been shaken. Rebuilding is a real challenge. The foundations of the relationship will have to be re-enforced and strengthened.

But before the restructuring begins, the partner who has broken the trust will need to prove that they recognise the damage that has been caused. The debris must be cleared before the couple can start rebuilding. This takes time, patience and determination from both parties. But it can be done.

Just as prevention is the best cure, so keeping mutual trust intact is the best way to have a healthy and happy relationship. If you are unhappy in your life with your partner, take action. Talk to one another. Make sure that each of you feels your needs are being met. Respect your partner's trust. Don't jeopardise the future of your relationship by being unfaithful.

The more you talk openly and honestly together, the more secure your relationship becomes. Talk about your worries and your fears. **Keep mutual respect and trust as the foundation stones of your relationship.**

Now get going on these tasks for Step Two and enjoy your journey of mutual discovery.

SESSION ONE

Your Ideal Partner

Even though you already have a partner, if you were to design your ideal, what qualities would you look for?

Sit down and make a list of what you would like to see in a life partner. Be as ambitious as you like, but be specific. For example, instead of writing, 'Someone who makes me happy', think of what personal attributes you admire most.

Now read over your list. How much of what you have written refers to physical attributes – height, weight, looks; and how much refers to personal qualities – kindness, sense of humour, gentleness, intelligence, integrity? If physical qualities dominate, then perhaps you should think again. Living with a film star can have its challenges too.

Next, go through your ideal partner list again. This time, number the qualities in order of importance to you. Which qualities do you consider essential in a life partner, and which are optional extras?

Now see how your partner measures up to your ideal standard. Tick the qualities that your partner has already shown. Where they fall short, stop and take note. How important is this in your order of priorities? Talk to your partner about this.

SESSION TWO

Part A

Sit down alone at the computer or with your special notebook and pen and answer the following questions. Spend a few minutes on each topic. If you think you have said it all in two words, stay with the topic and see if you can think of more details. Each assignment addresses a different aspect or perspective of this person you want to know so well.

1. What first attracted you to your partner?
2. What are their strengths?
3. What ambitions do they have?
4. Are there aspects of your partner that irritate or confuse you? Name them.
5. What interests do you share?
6. Write down your expectations for this relationship. You might include, for example, security, love, acceptance, respect, support or happiness. Now arrange your list in order of importance to you.
7. Which of your expectations are being met at the moment?
8. Do you consider your expectations reasonable or might you be depending on your partner to fulfil needs that only you can satisfy?
9. Name three qualities that your partner admires in you.
10. Name two changes in behaviour or attitude you think your partner would like you to make.
11. What causes stress for your partner?
12. How do they manage stress?
13. Is there mutual respect in your relationship?
14. Do you feel that you can always trust your partner?
15. How do you most often feel when you are with your partner?
16. What are your feelings about the future of this relationship?

Part B

Now arrange a time to talk together. Choose a situation where you will both feel relaxed and free from distractions. Discuss the questions you have answered above. Try to fill in the gaps in your knowledge of your partner. Maybe it has been a long time since you have discussed such issues, both for you as individuals and for you as a couple. So be prepared to give it time.

Even if your partner has not participated in the programme so far, they will be happy to know that you are interested in learning more about them.

SESSION THREE

Sharing Feedback from Stage One

Did your partner participate in Step One of the *Rekindle the Spark* programme? If so, this stage is easier for both of you. All you have to do now is share with each other what you wrote about yourselves in Step One. If you do not feel comfortable with the idea of sharing everything, read **Keeping Secrets** below.

If your partner has not joined in the programme yet, all is not lost. Agree on a quiet time together. Invite your partner to read your story. Then ask them some of the questions from Step One.

Sharing Is Caring – Some Tips on this Stage of the Programme

- Allow enough time to do this assignment properly – there is so much more to each story once you look closer.
- If you have not fully explored an issue together, agree on a time to address it again. It is really important not to rush things.
- Remember to be sensitive to each other's feelings here. People can have mixed emotions when looking back at their childhood, adolescence or early sexual experiences.
- Thank your partner for allowing you find out more about them.

Keeping Secrets

You and your partner are a couple. It is important that each of you respects the confidentiality of what the other shares. Confidentiality means avoiding the temptation to discuss particular issues with friends or extended family. You must be able to trust one another. Once you feel it is safe to trust each other, you can start to share your inner thoughts more fully.

How open have you been to date with your partner? If there are issues which you are not comfortable sharing with your partner, try to work out why. What would have to change to allow you to share your story? Ask yourself the question: *what is the worst thing that can happen if I tell them?*

Sit with that thought for a while. Identify your fears around revealing information about yourself. Are you afraid of being ridiculed, afraid that you will not seem so likeable? Once you have recognised the cause of your reluctance to share, you can talk to your partner about your fears.

You will probably find that, far from being disinterested, unsympathetic or disbelieving, your partner will be really grateful to you for opening up a bit more and will be most supportive. Their respect for you will grow. They will probably have guessed half the story already. That often happens when you have been sharing your lives for some time.

SESSION FOUR

Looking Ahead

Sit down together and set yourselves goals as a couple:

- What kind of life do you want to have together? Focus here on what you want rather than what you don't want.

- What do you want to have achieved in five or ten years' time? Be as ambitious here as you like – it is good to set yourselves imaginative goals.
- What do you both consider to be important? Agree on three priorities in your lives.
- Explore your similarities. It is good to acknowledge all you have in common.
- Acknowledge your differences. This shows that you respect each other as individuals.
- Can you each live with these differences? If not, why not? Variety is the spice of life. But if these differences seem unacceptable, see if you can reach a compromise.

Reality Check – Who's in Control?

Think about your attitude to your partner. Are you prepared to accept them as they are, or are you hoping to change some of the attributes that you don't like? Believing that you can change another person is a mistake. It will most likely lead to problems in the future. It is fine to challenge behaviour or attitudes that you don't like, but you should keep reminding yourself that ultimately, you are the only one who can change you. And the same goes for your partner. Neither of you is in charge of the other.

Feedback

How does it feel now that you have shared more of yourselves? Do you feel closer to your partner? Write your response in your notebook.

If the Going Gets Tough

Sometimes when you address differences, things seem to get harder before they improve. If you have gone through all the above exercises and feel somewhat overwhelmed, do not give up. You are doing something really valuable for your marriage.

There are **three** important reasons to stay with the *Rekindle the Spark* programme:

1. This is only one step of a ten-step programme. Each step helps you explore a different aspect of your relationship. Perhaps the main problem between you and your partner is one of poor communication; maybe it is how you handle arguments. The thing is, you really won't know how much your relationship can improve until you have completed the full programme.
2. Every step contains exercises and techniques to be used to address specific relationship problems. By the time you have completed the whole programme you will have the skills and the confidence to deal with future relationship problems should they arise.
3. Even if you think your relationship is over, I urge you to complete the *Rekindle the Spark* programme. Why? Because while you are dealing with the problems in this relationship, you are learning a lot about yourself and the choices you have made. This will help you avoid repeating the pattern in any future relationship.

Step Three

COMMUNICATION – GIVING THE MESSAGE

How well do you and your partner communicate with each other? How would you like things to be? In Step Three we look at how we give or send messages, both spoken and unspoken. Becoming aware of the subtle and perhaps not so subtle messages we convey to one another makes us more conscious of their impact. In this chapter you will be introduced to a unique tool for effective communication.

Communication Problems: The Number One Cause of Marital Breakdown

Did you know that research shows that poor communication is the most common cause of marriage and long-term relationship breakdown? This is not too surprising. Messages often get jumbled or misinterpreted, or even go unheard. You may think that you have explained yourself, but the listener may not have understood. You may think that certain things go without saying, but does the listener always get the unspoken message?

Communication within couples is therefore hugely important. If your partner does not receive the messages you are giving, then there cannot be mutual understanding. Let's start by looking at some of the most common statements regarding communication that I have encountered in my work as a relationship counsellor.

Common Communication Issues

- *My partner just doesn't understand me* – It is important to note the emphasis in this statement. Certainly, feeling misunderstood is never pleasant. But watch out for adopting the victim mentality. The implied message here is that if only your partner was better or changed in some way you would feel understood. Is this really fair? The question is: how easy is it for your partner to understand you? It takes two to communicate effectively.

- *I don't like to say what I really think* – While there is always a place for tact, it is vital that you communicate your thoughts to your life partner. Few of us are mind readers, so saying what you think by expressing your opinions clearly is essential. Of course timing is important here, especially if you are concerned about upsetting your partner.

- *We cannot find space in our lives to just sit and chat* – Note the wording here: the message is that time has been lost and can't be found. How about MAKING time instead of finding it? You make time to work, eat and look after others. So why not make time to be with the most important person in your life?

- *We're not able to discuss anything without a row developing* – This is a common complaint when a couple has developed poor communication patterns. We are all creatures of habit, so we tend to repeat behaviour even when it is negative. Maybe you find that it is just one no-go issue that fuels an argument or perhaps rows have become increasingly frequent. Next time you start a discussion, try to be more aware of negativity in your attitude and even in your body language.

- *I wouldn't dream of discussing that with my partner* – If this is the case, ask yourself why. Would it feel safe to share some of your hidden self with your partner? Do you think that your partner would feel safe to share with you? Confidentiality is a wonderful gift to give your partner. It means you can share more intimately with one another. And once confidentiality is established in your marriage you realise that there will be no more secrets between you.

The Three Components of Communication

The *Oxford English Dictionary* tells us that to communicate is to transmit or pass on, impart or convey information. But how do we succeed in achieving effective communication? What is the best way to evoke understanding? There are three essential stages in communication:

1. Giving the message
2. Receiving the message
3. Understanding the message

Here in Step Three of the programme we will focus on the first component – how we convey or express messages. The other two elements – receiving and understanding the message – will be discussed in Step Four.

We give messages all the time. Next time you go down the street, observe the people passing by. Note their body language. Do some people walk tall with confidence while others scurry by? Then look at the facial expressions. No doubt they range from open, smiling faces to closed or pained expressions. What messages have you received? And all this has been noted before you even hear a word.

So when it comes to communicating with your partner, it is good to become more aware of all the unspoken messages you give one another.

Becoming Aware of Non-Verbal Messages

Body Language

We can communicate both positive and negative messages very effectively through body language. Open arms, standing tall, a secret nudge, making eye contact say so much. Conversely, folded arms, slouching, a shrug of indifference, stiffening your shoulders at your partner's approach, looking away to avoid eye contact all carry their own negative messages.

Facial Expression

No doubt by now you are both experts at reading one another's unspoken messages. Our faces can give the clearest yet most subtle messages of all. You can feel so heartened by a smile, a wink, a loving look from your beloved, and so disheartened by a frown, a scowl, a rolling of eyes, a hostile stare. It is amazing to experience the power of a raised eyebrow, of 'that look', and then the magic of an intimate glance, a secret unspoken 'I love you.'

Behaviour and Attitude

Think of how you are when you feel excited and happy. Do you have a skip in your step? Do you do little acts of kindness for your spouse? Do you laugh and look on the bright side of life? Do you feel grateful for simple pleasures?

Now let's reverse the coin. When you feel down, angry or irritated what happens? Do you tend to revert to what I call the *3S's – sighing, sulking* and *silence?* Each of these behaviours conveys a distinct but corrosive message.

Sighing, even inwardly, indicates a negative attitude. When someone sighs, it sets a tone of resignation, a reluctance to engage, a message that says 'Do I really have to talk to you?' If you have a tendency to sigh, the best approach is first of all to sort out what exactly you are feeling. Once you can identify your own feeling, name it to yourself. Does your feeling say more about you than about your partner? Think about it. Then stop sighing.

Sulking also sends out a very negative message. It implies that you are the wounded one, the victim. Therefore you feel exonerated from having to make any effort to set things right. It is up to your partner to do all the work. Prolonged sulking builds a wall of silence between you.

Silence, also called stonewalling, is one of the most damaging behaviours of all. Renowned American psychologist John Gottman cites stonewalling as one of what he calls 'the four horsemen of the Apocalypse'. He recognises its potential to wreak havoc in a relationship. Just think what it would feel like to be stonewalled. The messages conveyed by silence include:

- I'm not interested in you.
- You are not important to me.
- We are not on the same team.
- You're not worth bothering about.
- You're useless.

Important message to all couples: silence is a form of emotional abuse; it is disrespectful to your spouse; it is unworthy of a loving couple.

Getting It Right: Communicating Verbal Messages Effectively

Now that you are more conscious of how you and your partner communicate non-verbally, it is time to look at how you communicate with words.

With the multiple ways of connecting people available to us today, it is amazing to realise that effective and meaningful communication is still such a challenge. Despite the texts, emails and smartphones, it can still be difficult to access the right words to express your deepest thoughts and feelings.

Many couples find that they struggle to keep in touch at a deep level with one another. There is so much to be done always. They cannot seem to find the time. Other couples, frustrated that each effort at communication ends in a row, communicate less and less. One day one of them decides to resort to silence. They now only communicate when absolutely necessary. As we have already discussed, this silence is a sinister and damaging tactic. It pervades their home, their lives, their very souls. It is utterly destructive to a relationship.

Women and Men

From my over twenty years of experience in counselling, certain patterns have emerged in how women and men perceive communication problems. These are simply observed comments and are not in any way definitive. Read them and see what you think.

What women say:

- He doesn't listen to me.
- I want him to understand my feelings more.
- I want empathy from him, not logic.
- I'm looking for connection, for sharing.
- Rows should be about trying to understand each other, not about blame.
- I want us both to feel that we're on the same team.

What men say:

- She's too emotional.
- I don't need to know all her feelings.
- Just tell me the problem and I'll try to fix it.
- When she complains I want to switch off.
- Rows should not be about winning or losing, about who's right and who's wrong.
- I want us both to feel that we're on the same team.

Can you identify with some of these comments? What does your partner think?

Let's start with what men and women have in common. Both parties agree that rows should not be divisive; they should not be about being right or wrong, or about blame. This is significant so try bearing it in mind next time there is a row brewing. They also agree on the importance of being on the same team. There is no doubt that this is of fundamental significance in a marriage. It means that even when you are at odds with one another, no one doubts that you are committed to working together to solve whatever issues arise. It means that you each know that your partner is ultimately the person to help you be your best self.

Now let's look at the differences in the comments above. Do you see that there is a difference in perspective? Women tend to look for empathy, for emotional support; men tend to be more pragmatic and rational.

There is much ongoing debate among psychologists regarding brain differences between genders, but the prevailing consensus is that males use the left brain, which controls logic, information, reasoning and action, before engaging the right brain, which controls sensory and emotional perception. The result is that a man tends to be rational before he is emotional – *just tell me the problem and I'll try to fix it.*

In women, it is the reverse. Women tend to engage the right hemisphere of the brain, which controls intuition, insight and feelings, before the left or logical side. In practice, it means that women want their emotions to be acknowledged before they can engage in a rational discussion – *I want him to understand my feelings more.*

Of course there are many exceptions to such generalisations, but it is sometimes helpful to bear these gender characteristics in mind.

WITT – The Secret of Effective Communication

And now to introduce you to my special technique – I call it **WITT**. This is a really powerful tool to have in your communication kit. Like all skills and techniques, it requires conscious effort and practice before it becomes part of your automatic response system. But once mastered, it will ease your path in life. Using this key to effective communication will have a positive effect on your relationship not just with your life partner but with everyone else too.

W – Words
I   – Information
T – Tone
T – Timing

Words

There are so many ways to convey our thoughts and feelings. But most of them are inadequate. Choosing the right words to say what you really mean is an art in itself. And it is in this area of feelings that language lets us down most of all. So before embarking on a complaint, for example, sort out what exactly it is that you want to convey. Let us take an example.

Case Study

Peter and Jane are a young couple who have been married for eight years. They have a history of frequent rows which they both find upsetting. Peter has just returned from work. He does not appear to have Jane's dress, which she had asked him to collect from the dry cleaners. She had planned to wear it to her sister's hen party tonight. Before following *Rekindle the Spark*, Jane would have started by attacking Peter:

'I knew you'd forget. You're so stupid!'

Once Peter feels under attack, he goes on the defensive:

'What do you mean "stupid"? Just because I forgot to pick up your stupid dress.'

The attack approach can also invite a counterattack: *'Well at least I'm not as stupid as you are!'*

Instead of going on the attack, Jane asks Peter about the dress in a non-confrontational way, opening the discussion with a question. This can avoid misunderstanding. She simply asks:

'Did you remember to collect my dress?'

When she hears that Peter has indeed forgotten to collect it, Jane takes a deep breath so as not to overreact. She then tells him how she feels about it:

'Oh no. I am really disappointed that you forgot.'

She knows that she has a tendency to be dramatic, so she tries to put the issue into perspective – it is not, after all, the end of the world.

Peter now understands Jane's viewpoint more fully. He is thankful that this has not escalated into a major row. Instead of being defensive, he apologises and offers to go back and pick up the dress. This is indeed progress.

So in summary, when you are upset with your partner:

- Choose words which are not emotive.
- Ask a question rather than make an accusation.
- Name your feelings rather than label your partner.
- Keep things in perspective.

Information

The core question here is what do you want to convey to your partner – is it how you feel, is it something you want to see happen or is it simply factual information which you need to share?

A really effective exercise is to spend some time thinking about what you want to say. Think through the incident or issue; work out your feelings. Sometimes you may feel very strongly about something not due to the issue itself but because it reminds you of a similar situation from your past. Think about this. Can you sort out your actual feelings about the issue to hand? Then prioritise – distinguish between what is truly important and what is not. Now decide on what you want your partner to know.

Another pitfall in choosing what you want to convey is the temptation to go off course. Back to Peter and Jane. There is no point in Jane adding:

'This is not the first time you've forgotten to do things for me. Remember two weeks ago you forgot to pick me up when I left the car in to be serviced. It was so embarrassing – I had to take a taxi in the end. You just never think of me.'

I call this the pile-up approach. Feeling that you're the injured and innocent party sometimes brings a sense of entitlement to add in past injuries. Soon there is an almost insurmountable heap of baggage between you. So keep it simple – stick to the incident in hand.

Tone

'Thanks so much.'

Try saying these three words in different tones of voice to convey different meanings. How many variations can you achieve?

There are three components to spoken language which constitute tone: the note or *pitch* of the voice, the *inflection* (is the voice rising or falling as the sentence ends?) and the *feeling* being expressed. Back to *'Thanks so much.'* Those three words can express sincerity, gratitude, nonchalance, sarcasm or even anger, depending on how they are spoken. Yet the words themselves have not changed.

So before you next broach a sensitive issue with your partner, decide on the tone of voice you are going to use. A calm, non-confrontational tone can have a big impact on the message you give to your partner.

Timing

This is a real challenge. If you are upset with your partner, there is not much point in a throwaway caustic comment as you run out the door. This just ensures that you will both feel confused and angry until the matter is discussed properly. Sometimes the opportunity to talk just presents itself but more often there is a need for dedicated time. So choose a quiet time to address an issue.

When you know there is a sensitive topic that needs to be discussed, the first thing to do is acknowledge it. Try saying something like:

'I know we need to talk about this, but I'm under pressure right now. How about this evening after dinner?'

Not only have your partner's concerns been acknowledged, but you have also committed to an appointed time to discuss the matter. Your partner already feels a bit better because they have been shown respect.

A Word of Warning

Where possible, avoid addressing an issue in anger. Heightened feelings make us more emotional and therefore less rational. Better to wait until you have cooled down so that you can both talk in a more rational way. This is another good reason to schedule dedicated time to talk.

SESSION ONE

When you next feel upset with your partner over any issue, follow the steps below:

1. Stop. Think before you speak. Identify your dominant feeling – do you feel hurt, furious, anxious, appalled? Live with the feeling for a while. Put your level of upset on a scale of 1–10.
2. Go back over the incident in your mind. What made you react negatively? Do you think your partner is aware of the depth of your feelings? (Remember, you have not spoken yet.)
3. Wait. Allowing some distance between the incident and the feedback will make for better communication. Think back over the incident and your reaction to it once more. How do you feel now? Has your level of upset decreased? If so, it is time to talk to your partner.
4. Use your WITT with as much care as you can manage. Choose a time when you can both be attentive. Say, *'I would like to talk to you about something important. When would suit you?'*
5. Choose words which are factual, e.g. *'I felt hurt when you ….'* Avoid using emotive language, e.g. *'How dare you speak to me like that! I was never so insulted in all my life!'*
6. Remember to keep your tone of voice as calm and non-accusatory as possible.
7. Ask your partner to recount the incident as they see it.
8. Can you now understand how your partner felt?
9. How do you feel about the issue now?

Trouble-Shooting Guide

We are still having rows when we try to discuss an issue.

- Do a take two of Session One with your partner.
- How might the discussion have been handled better last time?
- Be open to constructive criticism from your partner.

We both still tend to get angry when we talk.

- What is the ingredient in the way you communicate that most irritates your partner?
- Try to identify the triggers for your own annoyance – certain words, gestures, tone of voice?
- This is a two-way system. So be open to receiving your partner's message even if it is negative. Then they will do the same for you.

My partner still does not get my messages.

- If your partner seems to misinterpret what you say, you should reconsider the words you have used.
- To explain more accurately what you mean, name a feeling or give an example.
- If things are still confused, avoid reacting with anger – after all, your partner is only reacting to the words you have used. Staying calm can help get the message across.
- Don't take a misunderstanding as a personal insult. Try to understand the message your partner is giving you.

ONGOING EXERCISE

Observe how you address your partner. Become more conscious of using your WITT. With practice, you will both be more in tune with each other. You will learn to communicate without offending or setting off sensitive triggers.

Step Four

THE ELUSIVE ART OF TRULY LISTENING

Recap: The Three Components of Communication

1. Giving the message
2. Receiving the message
3. Understanding the message

In Step Three we discussed how we give messages. Here in Step Four we look first at how you and your partner receive the messages that have been conveyed. We then focus on understanding those messages.

Do you ever feel that your partner does not really listen to you? Well, don't worry – you are not alone. And chances are that at times your partner feels the very same.

For most of us, the art of true listening is a real challenge. Yet good, attentive listening is a vital ingredient in a healthy relationship. That is why Step Four focuses on this very important area.

You may want to feel that your partner listens to you, but are you a good listener? If you can master the art of true listening, your partner can learn from you. How do you become a good listener? Read on and find out. By the end of Step Four, you should be equipped with all the necessary tools.

To truly listen to the other person requires *real concentration and focus*. Your ability to listen attentively can depend on your perception of what is being said. Good listening also demands a receptive mind, open to receiving whatever message is being given.

Feeling Unheard

What is it like for you to feel unheard? The couples I have worked with report a wide range of experiences:

- I feel worthless, as if I'm not even worth listening to.
- I feel really frustrated – no matter what I say, I can't get the message across.
- After a while I become withdrawn.
- I think my partner is not interested in me.
- Eventually, I become really angry.

What do you experience when you feel unheard? How does feeling unheard affect your partner?

Becoming Aware of Your Abilities as a Listener

Next time your partner starts to discuss a sensitive issue with you, try to observe how you react. Take note of how you are feeling. Your reaction can depend on the tone of voice your partner uses, or on your anticipation of what is going to be said.

- If it seems that you are being accused, you may feel that you are under attack. In this case you will only half listen – you will be busy preparing arguments for your defence.
- Or perhaps you tend to listen to your partner in the hope of finding a perceived error in what is being said. This means that you will start your response by correcting your partner rather than addressing the issues that have been raised.
- Maybe you and your partner have not been getting along well recently. You think that the complaints have become predictable. In that case, you may have got into a habit of discounting what your partner says even before they speak. If so, try to imagine what being ignored feels like for your partner.

Receiving Unexpected Messages

As you are in a long-term relationship, you have naturally built up a mental picture of your partner as a certain type of person. This is based on what you have experienced together so far. Your image of your partner is also based on your life experiences to date. As time goes by and you get to know each other better, you expect your partner to react in certain ways and to say certain things.

If your partner steps out of that image, if they say something to you that is totally unexpected, you may react in one of the following ways:

- You might ignore the message or pretend you have not heard. What has been said has made you feel too uncomfortable.
- You may be unwilling to receive the message so you block it out completely.
- Perhaps you decide to deal with the message by excusing it. You tell yourself that this was just a mistake – your partner could not have really meant what was said.
- You might react with nervous laughter – you decide to dismiss the remark as a joke.

When you receive an unexpected and even unwelcome message from your partner, the best option is, of course, to listen carefully. This will probably mean asking them to repeat what has been said so that you really get the message. It is especially important that you receive and acknowledge an unexpected or challenging communication. This is how you get to know yourself and your partner more deeply.

When a Message Goes Unheard

What does your partner do if you refuse to listen? It may have taken quite a bit of courage to give this message in the first place. Maybe it was given as a result of growing frustration – other, more subtle messages given to date have not been received. Now this message, spoken clearly, is being ignored. The results can be damaging to the relationship.

Your partner may decide not to try giving you the message again. There is no point, they feel. The feelings of frustration, resentment or anger are now left unarticulated by your partner. But they do not go away. They only fester and seethe until they bubble over one day, with possibly serious consequences.

Or your partner may decide to repeat the message in the hope that you will listen. With each repetition the anger and frustration grow. This can make the language used more and more emotive. You then can feel under attack and so go on the defensive. Your partner's chances of being listened to are now slim indeed.

Getting the Message Across

'How can I get my partner to listen to me?'

This is a common plea. The frustration at being ignored can build up into feelings of anger and rejection. For you to operate effectively as a couple, each needs to feel listened to. Each of you needs to feel that your message has been heard by the other.

Before you and your partner do the listening exercise in this section, assess yourself as a listener. Do you only half listen? Some of the pitfalls mentioned below ring true for most people. Which of them apply to you?

Pitfalls of Poor Listening and How to Avoid Them

- *Switching off once you think you are going hear a complaint – 'Here we go again'*
  - Maybe the message should not be dismissed. Give your partner a chance.
- *Interrupting your partner to make a correction to the story*
  - Hold it – your chance will come later.
- *Filtering out negative messages – a common self-protection device*
  - Stay calm and listen.
- *Preparing your defence while your partner is speaking*
  - This shows that you are thinking of yourself. Try to think more of your partner.

- *Failing to pick up your partner's feelings of hurt, frustration or anger*
  - Focus on the feelings behind your partner's words. Watch their body language.
- *Dismissing the message even before you have heard it*
  - Try opening your mind before you close it.

Watch Out for these Tell-Tale Statements – They Can Become a Habit

- *'But wait a minute ...'* – This indicates that you are on the *defensive*. You are already prepared with a counterattack.
- *'I can't believe I'm hearing this ...'* – This response of *outrage*, mock outrage or anger indicates that you are refusing to listen.
- *'Oh for heaven's sake! That's what you always say.'* – This *dismissive* response expresses contempt. It indicates that you have little respect for what your partner feels or thinks.

Each of these responses is a clear indication of poor listening and can only have a negative impact on your relationship with your partner. As you become more aware of how you speak and listen to one another, you will no doubt avoid using such tactics.

We are all guilty of poor listening at times. Yet we all want to be heard. So how can we cultivate good listening habits? Listed below are the qualities of good listening that you should aim for. They are not very complicated – all you need to do is practise until these traits come naturally when your partner is speaking to you.

To Be a Good Listener

- Clear your mind of distractions.
- Put aside any negative thoughts such as irritation or anger.

- Look at your partner when they are speaking.
- Watch out for signs of distress or frustration.
- Try to focus only on what is being said, not on your reply.
- Keep an open mind even if you don't like what you hear.
- Try to empathise with what your partner is saying.

What do you need to change to make you a better listener? Work on it.

SESSION ONE

Exercise – Am I a Good Listener?

Read the following questions and write your responses in your notebook. Are there areas where you could improve as a listener?

1. Do you try to clear your mind of other distracting thoughts when your partner speaks to you?
2. Are you good at focusing on what your partner is saying?
3. Can you accept what your partner says with an open mind?
4. Do you think you are good at assessing your partner's feelings?
5. Can you feel empathy with what your partner is feeling?
6. If your partner talks angrily to you can you listen to what they are saying?
7. If your partner is talking about an issue that is important to them, do you take time to listen to what is being said?
8. How often do you and your partner have a meaningful chat, away from IT, children or other distractions?
9. Do you think your partner shares their innermost feelings and secrets with you?

SESSION TWO

The challenge here is contained in a listening exercise. This exercise is designed to help you and your partner really listen to one another.

Listening Exercise – Instructions

Allow at least one hour of dedicated time free from distractions. *N.B. Don't forget to put your phones on silent.*

You will each get an opportunity to speak and be heard. Whoever speaks first is Person A. Whoever listens first is Person B. Read the guidelines before starting the exercise.

Person A Guidelines

- As you talk about the incident/issue that you found upsetting, focus on how it made you *feel*.

   For example: *'When you didn't arrive on time, I felt let down at first. As the time passed I became angry. But when I couldn't contact you I began to feel anxious for your safety. Then finally you breezed in with some feeble excuse for being late. I felt relieved to see you but really hurt and still angry. You dismissed my upset, telling me to cheer up – now that you had arrived we should enjoy our time together. I tried to move on but all evening I felt resentful, as if you did not understand me at all.'*

Person B Guidelines

- As you listen, focus only on what your partner is saying. Take particular note of how this incident made your partner feel.
- When giving your feedback, stick as closely as you can to what your partner has said.

- Avoid dismissing your partner's feelings – e.g. *'You shouldn't feel hurt.'* What your partner feels is what your partner feels – it is real for them and must be acknowledged.
- Avoid corrections – e.g. *'You said I was half an hour late. In fact I was just 20 minutes late.'* This indicates that while you were listening you were preparing your defence. It reinforces your partner's sense of not being heard and understood.

Listening Exercise – Part One

- Person A speaks for five minutes without interruption on an issue that they have found annoying or troubling in the relationship. Person B keeps silent. **You must listen without interrupting** – even if you think Person A has got the story all wrong.
- Person B then spends three minutes recounting as accurately as possible what they have heard Person A say. This is simply recording – no corrections or perceived inaccuracies to be addressed at this stage. You simply say: *'What I have heard you say is …'.*
- Person A gets one minute to correct any misinterpretations or omissions that Person B has made: *'Yes you got most of it right. But you left out that I said I felt hurt, sad …'.*
- The object of the exercise here is that Person A feels that Person B has really heard what Person A has said and that Person B acknowledges how Person A feels. So when you are the listener (Person B) it is vital that you simply acknowledge receipt of the information.
- Avoid giving your response, however well meant – e.g. *'I know you say it makes you angry but really there is no need to feel that way.'*

There will be time later to come to an agreement on how to handle such an issue in the future. For now, your role as listener is to do exactly that – LISTEN

– not to comment, however helpful you may think that could be.

Listening Exercise – Part Two

Next, the roles are reversed. Now Person B gets a chance to speak on an aspect of the relationship. It can be on the same issue or it might be something else. Person B decides. Follow the steps as in Part One.

Feedback

- Check – did you both feel listened to after the two sessions?
- Has each of you acknowledged the feelings of the other?
- If so, it is now hopefully possible to move towards a solution.
- Try to stay open to the suggestions of your partner.
- The solution may involve a change in behaviour patterns, attitude or perception.
- You might also agree to raise a difficult issue sooner next time one of you feels upset or hurt.
- This exercise should leave each person feeling better understood.

I hope that by now you feel better equipped with tools for conflict resolution.

WARNING – THIS EXERCISE IS MORE DIFFICULT THAN IT FIRST APPEARS. SO KEEP UP THESE LISTENING EXERCISES.

Understanding the Message

We have now reached the third component of communication: understanding, getting, interpreting and accepting the message. Easier said than done, you may say. Here we look at some potential obstacles that can hamper our interpretation of what we hear.

Challenging Perceptions

Did you ever have the experience of hearing someone being interviewed, let's say on radio or television? You are quite impressed with what you hear. The person sounds balanced and fair. However, later you meet a friend who has heard the same interview and has a very different opinion of the interviewee.

'What an obnoxious man', she storms. *'I certainly would not trust him one bit.'*

Of course we all are entitled to have different opinions. But there is something more going on here. Each of you has reacted according to your own values, interests and past experiences.

So which of you is right? This is not a question of being right or wrong but of trying to understand as accurately as possible the message the speaker wants to convey. When we hear a message that correlates with our own ideas, we are naturally pleased with the endorsement. When the message does not correspond with what we perceive as accurate or right, when the message is not what we want to hear, it presents us with a real challenge.

Take the story of five people looking at a horse in a field. The first person sees a fine racing horse; the second sees a good farm horse; the third sees a potential family pet; the fourth sees a beautiful photo opportunity; the fifth sees a dangerous animal that could kill you. The horse is still itself – but each person sees something that is coloured by their knowledge (or lack of it), their interests and their experience.

So if your partner suggests that you are taking up a message the wrong way, be prepared to acknowledge that maybe they meant something very different to what you perceived as the intended communication. If you tend to get very upset when your partner does not wish to upset you, perhaps it is worth exploring what triggers your negative perception. Maybe that horse is a beautiful photo opportunity and not a lethal aminal after all.

Recognising and Removing Our Filters

To assess how well you understand what is being said, it is also helpful to become aware of filters. Filters in this context are the preconceived notions or prejudices that we carry within ourselves. These filters colour the lens through which we view the world. Our family background and cultural beliefs have a strong influence on how we react in certain situations.

Case Study

Meet John and Mary. They have been married for eleven years and have three children. Theirs is a good relationship until it comes to their social life. They have great friends in the neighbourhood and have enjoyed many evenings in their homes. But as soon as John mentions having anyone back to their house, Mary comes up with one excuse after another. This surprises John as Mary is a great cook. Anyway, he argues, they could have a barbecue, which John would prepare. But Mary is still reluctant.

'I notice that as soon as I mention inviting guests to our house you become tense, Mary. What is it that you're afraid of?'

'I'm not really sure', Mary says. 'I suppose I don't like people prying into our private lives, poking their noses around our home.'

'But these are our friends, Mary. We've been to their houses so often. You enjoy their company. Surely you can trust them not to pry.'

Mary thinks for a while and then says, 'Maybe you're right, John. They are our friends and I suppose I do trust them. It's just that my mother always said that the only reason people ask to go to the bathroom in your house is because they want to snoop around upstairs. Now that I think about it, that's kind of illogical. Anyway, we have a downstairs cloakroom.'

Once Mary becomes aware of her prejudice or filter, she can remove it.

We are usually unaware of our prejudices until they are pointed out to us. And it often takes a partner to do that. Once you become aware of a bias you can assess it. Ask yourself – is my prejudice based on fear or ignorance? Do I have this negative reaction because of messages I received in childhood?

It is good to be challenged from time to time. If your attitude seems irrational, if it is based on an inherited prejudice, it is worth reassessing. Ask yourself, *'Can I remove this filter? Can I move on from this prejudice?'*

Once we can see things as they really are, and not coloured by filters, we can open our minds more fully to understanding the messages we receive.

Clarifying

You have listened very carefully to your partner, you have tried to accept what has been said without prejudice, but you still can't quite understand or get the message. What next?

When this happens it is good to consider the words your partner has used. A word or phrase can mean two very different things to different people. When your partner says that they 'often' feel angry, it is worth clarifying what that means. How often is 'often'? Does it mean once a day? Once a week? Taking time to clarify what exactly your partner wishes to say will avoid the possibility of misinterpretation and hence misunderstanding.

Considering Your Response

Only now that you have really got the message is it time to start considering your response. Just remember to use your WITT.

You may think that this is a long and drawn-out process, but let me assure you that, with practice, these listening skills will become automatic. And once you both experience the relief and satisfaction of being truly acknowledged and heard, there will be no desire to return to old habits.

Step Five

RECOGNISING AND DEALING WITH FEELINGS

'How are you feeling?'
'I'm ok thanks. And you?'
'Fine. I'm fine.'

What are these two people really feeling? It is impossible for us to know because neither of them has named a feeling. Of course this happens all the time. You are hardly going to share your innermost feelings with everyone who asks.

But with your partner it needs to be different. Your partner deserves and wants to know how you are feeling inside. Words like 'ok' and 'fine' say nothing about what you are really thinking.

In Step Five you will be introduced to the various challenges that people experience when dealing with their feelings. Sometimes it can be hard to know what exactly is going on inside your head – maybe you are confused and find it difficult to express what you feel. Once you can identify the unspoken messages from your past environment, you will be able to decide if your way of handling your feelings is good for you and your relationship with your partner.

Thinking Around Feelings: Messages from Childhood

Expressing emotions openly is not easy for everyone. It can depend on your cultural background. In some cultures the open expression of feelings is quite acceptable and indeed expected. In others that is not the case. As you grow and develop, your environment dictates what behaviour is expected.

From a young age, we are taught how to respond to and express emotions. It is interesting to look at your role models as you grew up and see how they dealt with their feelings. The unspoken message might have been that expressing feelings was self-indulgent, or a form of attention-seeking. In that case, you may still tend to ignore your feelings and hence ignore your emotional needs. This, in turn, can make it difficult to bond emotionally with your partner. If, on the other hand, you were raised in an environment where you were the centre of attention you may tend to over-indulge in the expression of your emotions and think that the only feelings that matter are yours. That too can make life difficult for your partner. Most people, however, fall somewhere in between these two extremes.

Big Boys Don't Cry – Cultural Context

There can also be a gender bias regarding the expression of emotion. 'Big boys don't cry' has had a hugely repressive effect on generations of men in many cultures. The message here is clear. Boys must learn to repress rather than express their feelings. The sub-text is that the expression of emotion is considered non-masculine. In this cultural context, only girls are allowed to cry. And crying can be used to express almost every emotion – sadness, joy, anger, frustration, loneliness, rejection or fear.

So it is really not surprising that many people, especially men who have been brought up in an emotionally repressive environment, have difficulty in recognising and expressing their feelings, even with their life partners. The thinking and behaviour from childhood has to be unravelled before they can move on to feeling comfortable with their emotional side.

If there is difficulty in naming and expressing emotion in a healthy way, the default position is often anger. In this case repressed feelings cannot be identified or articulated. The resulting tension builds up and then boils over into an uncontrolled outburst of anger.

Anger and How to Deal with It

Recent research carried out by the British Association of Anger Management reveals that anger is cited as the main cause of breakup in 20 per cent of separated couples in the UK. That is quite a wakeup call to those who allow their anger control them. So let's take a closer look at this powerful emotion.

The first important point to make is that *it's OK to feel angry*. Anger is a normal human emotion and can be quite justifiable at times. It is how we manage it that counts. At a pre-verbal stage we can experience anger as primal animal rage. It is almost impossible to negotiate with a toddler throwing a tantrum. We must wait until their anger subsides before engaging with them in any rational way. As we mature into adulthood we acquire better skills to deal with the rush of adrenalin caused by sudden anger.

What Fuels Anger?

Anger is usually related to feeling stressed. The onset can be sudden or there may be a slow build-up. It is good to be able to identify the situations or circumstances that cause you stress. The range of triggers or stressors is endless: being overlooked, discounted, dismissed; feeling that your needs are not being met; fear of losing connection, of being separated from a source of comfort. Can you identify your triggers? Write them down in your notebook.

So What Happens When You Get Angry?

Think first of the *physiological effects*. Pallor or feeling hot, accelerated heart rate, blood pressure elevation, clenching fists, muscles tightening, changes in breathing, feeling that your head is going to burst, adrenalin rush, wanting to fight or run away – these are some of the physiological changes that may occur with anger. It all adds up to a rather unhealthy state don't you think? The moral here is obvious: being angry is not good for you. Therefore you need to learn to control it.

Now let's look at anger's *psychological effects.* Because it is such a strong emotion, anger, if left unmanaged, can eclipse your ability to be logical. Once you become overly emotionally charged your ability to think rationally shuts down, albeit temporarily, much like the toddler having a temper tantrum.

As long as you continue in this state of heightened anger, there is a risk that you will say or do things that hurt or harm others. And the irony here is that the most common targets of your anger are those who are closest to you. Anger is most often taken out on a loved one.

Are You an Exploder or an Imploder?

Exploders tend to vent their anger with shouting or violence that is harmful both to themselves and others. They use words as weapons, lashing out insults and accusations that are hurtful and damaging. Those who resort to physical violence are, of course, committing a crime. *Imploders* repress their anger without addressing it. They shut down, become introspective and disappear into themselves. This break in communication leaves their partner feeling excluded, sad and helpless. So either way, by letting anger take over, you are damaging both yourself and your relationship with your partner.

Manage Your Anger in Five Steps

1. Take time out. Move away from the situation that fuelled your anger. Focus on your breathing – can you slow it down?
2. Learn the art of triage – stay with your heightened feelings and think through the incident. Is this really a crisis situation? If so, your anger will not help. Try to put the situation into perspective. Wait until you have brought your anger level down to three out of ten. Do you feel less flushed or agitated now?
3. Now look again at your anger. Is it the only emotion you are feeling or can you access a primary emotion lying underneath? Tell yourself, *'I know I'm angry, but what else am I feeling?'* The primary emotion might be fear, sadness or hurt.

4. Once you feel more in control of yourself, start formulating your reaction. Consider what you are going to say. To express anger in a healthy way requires that you speak about your own feelings in as calm a voice as you can manage. Respect your partner – no shouting, no verbal abuse.

5. A tendency to get angry easily often indicates a lack of self-esteem. When you have dealt with an incident of anger, take time to reflect on how you feel. If you have had an uncontrolled outburst of anger, you will most likely feel bad – you may be ashamed or upset with yourself. Now that you can think more rationally you realise that throwing tantrums is not worthy of any adult and especially not worthy of you. So your self-esteem gets another knock. Start working on your self-esteem by thinking more positively about yourself and others.

If anger management is an issue for you, the good news is that you can change your behaviour. Try to make these five steps part of your ongoing daily routine. Each time you manage your anger well, your self-esteem will grow.

Set yourself specific goals to manage and control your emotions next time you feel that adrenalin rush. Be kind to yourself – don't give up when things don't go according to plan. Putting these steps into effect takes time and patience. But know that you can achieve your goal once you feel positive and determined.

When Confronted by Anger

It can be a scary and disconcerting experience to be confronted by someone who is really angry. You may feel shock, hurt or outrage, and become quite angry yourself. Then the cycle continues. Both of you are angry now; both become irrational. The anger mounts, things get out of hand and off you go on the anger merry-go-round – except there is nothing merry about it. It is a downward spiral.

No one listens; no one feels heard; both parties feel injured. Nothing has been achieved.

Here are three steps to take when next confronted by anger:

1. Stay calm. This is a big challenge, especially if you are in the habit of making counterattacks. But know that keeping your head while others are losing theirs is a really powerful strategy. If only one voice is raised and you respond quietly and calmly, this will de-escalate the heightened tension.
2. Don't take it personally. Did you know that 99 per cent of what others say and do is about them and not about you? Think about this. When you are feeling happy and confident you are unlikely to get angry or say nasty things to others. But if you are feeling out of sorts you are more likely to be impatient or intolerant of others. So remember this: insults and put-downs belong to the speaker. They are a reflection of how they are feeling. They are not to be believed and accepted by you. Once you realise this, you will find that you can deflect the anger of others and stop their jibes from impacting on your sense of self.
3. Help access the primary emotion. If you can stay calm when your partner gets angry, if you realise that what is said to you reflects on them and not on you, then you will be able to help your partner access their primary emotion. Try saying, *'You sound very upset, even sad – this must be very difficult for you.'* Or, *'You sound like you feel quite hurt by this.'*

How We Deal with Feelings – Emotional v Rational

Read the case study below and see what you think.

Case Study

Nathan and Kate have been married for twelve years. They have three children and both work outside the home. They have a good relationship but they react differently under stress. For example, when one day Nathan reverses into a parked car he is absolutely furious. But he immediately sets about analysing the situation: the other car was so badly parked, small wonder he hit it. This is the second time his car has been scratched. How much is it going to cost him? Can he afford to pay for the damage to both cars without it affecting his no claims bonus?

As soon as Kate sees him walk in the door she knows he is upset. Her first reaction on hearing the cause is to comfort Nathan. How dreadful! How is he feeling? Was he very upset when it happened? But Nathan does not want either the sympathy or the hug that is offered. He wants to discuss the facts of the case as he sees them. Afterwards, when the incident and its implications have been analysed, Kate is allowed to give him emotional support.

Now let us backtrack and follow Kate when a similar incident occurs. Her first reaction is more one of shock than of fury. She feels like crying but tries to stay calm. She needs to talk to someone about what has happened. Perhaps they can help her locate the owner of the other car, or give her some advice. She spends quite a long time trying to find the owner of the car before deciding to write a note; Nathan had done that within two minutes of the incident. By the time she gets home, Kate feels totally drained by the stress.

Nathan's first reaction is to want to know exactly what happened, in chronological sequence. He has lots of questions: Was the other car parked properly? Who witnessed the incident? What did she write in the note? But before Kate can discuss things dispassionately, she needs to be consoled and comforted. Once her emotional needs are met, they can proceed to the facts of the matter.

N.B. Many people, both male and female, do not conform to this stereotype. The illustration serves only to highlight the distinction between our rational and emotional sides. After doing the exercise in Session Two, you will have a clearer idea of how each of you tends to react.

Recognising Your Feelings

Whatever your gender or background, there is no denying that you have an emotional side, a part of the self which reacts instinctively and sensitively to each experience. This aspect of your nature must be given expression if you are to develop as a complete human being. Children usually have no problem letting us know when they are happy or unhappy, even though they may not be able to pinpoint the exact emotion. But if they grow up in an environment where feelings are not named or dealt with, then they become inhibited adults.

We all need to be able to express our feelings, but first we must be able to acknowledge and name them. Strong emotions, such as joy or anger, are usually easier to recognise than more subtle emotions such as resentment or insecurity. Once you can identify your feelings, the next challenge is to communicate them to your partner.

If you find it easy to express your feelings, you are fortunate. Just be careful that you don't go overboard. You must ensure that you don't swamp your partner so much with your emotions that there seems to be no room for their feelings.

What If Your Partner Is Reluctant to Share Their Feelings?

To encourage a reluctant partner to talk about their feelings, it may be helpful to go through the following checklist:

- Does your partner have space to talk about their feelings? In this context, space means quiet time when you both feel relaxed. Be prepared to put your listening hat on.
- Does your partner feel relaxed enough to share with you? Do you apply too much pressure to talk about feelings? This can be a real turn-off for someone who feels uncomfortable talking about emotions. So go gently and slowly.
- Are you open to accepting what your partner tells you? Maybe you tend to say, 'Well there's no need to feel like that.' In that case your partner will feel unheard and misunderstood. We each need

to try to validate the feelings of the other. Your partner feels what they feel, whether or not you consider that they should.

- Or are you the needy person? Do you like nothing better than talking about yourself and what you are feeling? In this case you may place huge emotional demands on your partner. No matter how much attention and positive feedback you receive, it is never enough. Your spouse may be left feeling exhausted or emotionally drained – and less likely than ever to open up to you.

The ideal is obvious – you and your partner need to achieve an emotional balance. You each need to be able to recognise how the other is feeling. You need to be comfortable when talking to one another about your emotions.

SESSION ONE

Naming and Expressing Feelings

Take your time with this exercise. It may help to take some notes.

In order to express feelings effectively, we need to identify them. What is it like for you when you are happy? Firstly, become more aware of changes in your body. Do you walk with a lighter step? Do you smile more? Do you find yourself whistling a happy tune? Next, observe how being happy also affects your mind. Do you feel less stressed? Adopt a more positive outlook? Are you kinder in your attitude to others?

Once you become more in tune to the presence of positive feelings, you can now work on recognising some negative emotions. Watch out for the tendency to label all negative feelings as anger. Remember that in 90 per cent of cases anger is a secondary emotion – in other words, when feeling emotionally overwhelmed many people opt for the default position of anger. It is only when you calm down and take time to think things through that you recognise the underlying primary emotion – maybe you were feeling hurt, sad, afraid, resentful or abandoned.

So next time you start feeling overwhelmed – you know that rush of blood to the head, the faster heart rate? STOP. See if you can calm yourself down and recognise and name the primary or underlying emotion. The next step is to express or communicate what you are feeling. If that is a challenge, ask yourself the great question, *'What is the worst thing that could happen if I told my partner how I really feel?'*

Check here for childhood memories – was it ever unsafe to show too much emotion when you were growing up? If so, why not share those thoughts and memories with your partner? Do you feel that it is safe to do so now? If not, tell your partner of your concerns – are you fearful of not being understood? Are you worried about confidentiality? Do you still think that the expression of feelings is self-indulgent? Sit down and talk about it.

ONGOING EXERCISE

Work on becoming more aware of what you are feeling as you go through each day. Remember, it is ok to acknowledge your feelings even if they are not happy ones.

SESSION TWO

Find your quiet spot and quiet time alone, without your partner. Sit down with your notebook and pen. Think of an incident from your past involving you and another person that really upset you. This can be something that happened when you were a child or it can be a recent event.

1. Briefly describe the incident.
2. Are you able to recall how you reacted when it first occurred?
3. What did you do?
4. What were your feelings at the time?
5. How did you deal with those feelings?
6. Now that you are back there again in that time, are you aware of feeling any of these emotions again?
7. Can you name them? Think about anger, hurt, sadness, frustration, self-pity, disgust or humiliation. The list goes on.
8. Is there anything about your reaction to that past event that you would like to change?

If you have difficulty recognising any feelings associated with this incident, please try again. Either the event you chose did not have a significant impact on you in the first place, or you have not given yourself enough time to really focus on it and relive it. This time round, try to recall more detail. Can you describe the setting? Who were the main players?

Instead of writing, try drawing a picture of the incident. Drawing can often help you see a situation more clearly. Use coloured crayons if you have them. Don't worry about your artistic talent – just draw stick figures if you like. This is not an art contest.

Now look at your picture and answer the following questions:

1. What does it tell you?
2. Where are you in the picture – in the centre or on the outside?
3. How big are you compared to the others in the picture?
4. What colours have you chosen to use – light or dark?
5. Now fill in some speech bubbles. Who said what?
6. How did you react at the time?

7. How did the others involved react?
8. How do you feel about your reaction at the time?
9. Is there anything about the incident that makes you feel uncomfortable? If so, can you put a more precise feeling word on the discomfort – regret, shame, anger, self-pity, sadness or loneliness?
10. Put yourself back there once more. What might have helped you deal with those feelings?
11. Was there anyone to confide in?
12. What might you have said to a trusted person?
13. What might you have done then that you didn't do?

SESSION THREE

Sit down with your partner. If you have both done Session Two, this is a good time to share your stories. If your partner has not participated, ask them to tell you about an incident in the past that caused anxiety or hurt. Try to encourage your partner to name the emotions felt at the time.

Recognising Each Other's Feelings

Having completed this exercise, you are now hopefully more conscious of your own emotions. The next challenge is to start to become aware of your partner's feelings. Answer the following questions separately. Then discuss your answers with your partner.

- Do you think that you are good at reading your partner's feelings?
- What key signs of stress, anxiety, anger and hurt would you recognise in your partner?
- How do you react to them? Do you tend to ignore them rather than deal with them?
- How do you think your partner feels about that?

- How easy or difficult is it for each of you to express your feelings?
- How could you help each other to feel comfortable about acknowledging feelings?
- How does each of you express anger?
- Could each of you handle this better?
- What about positive feelings – love, joy, admiration? How do you both express these?
- Do you think you could convey positive feelings to each other more often?
- When was the last time you told your partner *'I really admire you for ...'* or *'What I really like about you is ...'*?

Take your time discussing these questions and answers with your partner.

Feedback

Do you and your partner feel more comfortable talking about your feelings? If yes, well done. If not, keep talking. Focus on your own feelings until you can recognise and name them. Then see if your partner can do the same.

Sharing Feelings

Shared feelings bring a great closeness between two people. Your life partner is, hopefully, the person to whom you feel closest. Knowing your partner's thoughts and deepest feelings creates a special bond. Does your spouse or partner know your deepest feelings – what makes you feel excited; what brings you joy; your sorrows and your fears? Do you know the same about your spouse or partner? Think about this for a moment. If you don't know each other's intimate thoughts and feelings, why not start working on this today?

Step Six

THE OTHER PERSPECTIVE AND HOW TO HANDLE AN ARGUMENT

You are now past the halfway mark of the *Rekindle the Spark* programme. This is a good time to have a look at just how far you and your partner have come since you started out. You will by now, hopefully, be aware of an improvement in your ability to *communicate effectively*.

What have you noticed from the listening exercise in Step Four? Did the enforced silence of *truly listening* give you a greater insight into the thoughts and feelings of your spouse? If so, that means that you have started on the road to looking at life from another viewpoint or perspective. And this is what Step Six is all about. I have combined the topic of the other perspective with that of how to handle an argument because, of course, the best way to resolve disagreements is to be open to seeing the issue from another person's point of view.

Step Six helps you to look at and assess your ideas, especially the strongly held beliefs that can be a source of disagreement with your partner. I hope that Amanda and Karl's story will help you identify some of these issues and show how you and your partner can prevent your differences from having a negative effect on your relationship.

No two people think alike about everything. It would be worrying if that were the case. So it is only natural that you and your partner differ in your attitudes to certain issues. That is part of what makes your relationship exciting. However, there can be times when you and your partner fail to agree on something that you regard as

important. The issue may be one of attitude or behaviour. Perhaps you have different approaches to spending money; perhaps it is that your partner spends what you consider to be too much time out with friends. But no matter what the issue is, you know that you and your partner see it from different angles or perspectives.

Acquiring Attitudes

Did you ever stop to think how you acquired your core values and beliefs? As a child no doubt you bought into the attitudes and beliefs of your family. Then as you got older perhaps you began to question these and came up with your own belief system. As a teenager or young adult, each relationship you developed was based to some extent on shared attitudes and values. If there was little common ground, the relationship probably did not last very long. Some of these relationships may have caused you to re-assess your own beliefs – to re-arrange your own order of priorities in life. This is part of your healthy development as a mature person with your own integrity.

Challenging Attitudes

Now that you are in a committed relationship you may find that you have some firmly held beliefs around issues that your partner considers unimportant or even foolish. How do you handle this clash of attitudes? Perhaps you find it really difficult to get your partner to appreciate how important this issue is to you. Let's paint a possible scenario:

- You raise the issue and challenge your partner's attitude to it.
- Your partner responds with a teasing approach. But that only makes you feel misunderstood.
- You then perhaps try to explain your point of view – but your partner is not convinced.
- You now get emotional – after all, this is an important issue for you.

- Your partner reacts to the heightened emotion and before long you are involved in a full-blown row.
- You finish up even further away from reaching an understanding.

How can you get your partner to see this issue from your perspective?

Challenging Behaviour

It is not just differences in attitude that can be a source of tension in a relationship. Different priorities and behaviours may have an impact on your lives at home. Perhaps your partner considers keeping fit a priority. So they spend increasingly long periods away from home pursuing a chosen sporting activity. In this case you may start to feel neglected, deserted, unappreciated. You can see how much your partner enjoys the time out.

'But what about me?' you say. *'Where do I fit into this great keep-fit programme of yours?'*

If your partner's passion involves time spent at home, it can also present a challenge. Perhaps it is watching what you consider to be an excessive amount of television. Perhaps it involves being constantly on the computer, playing games online or following social media. In any case resentment can build up. You feel that your partner, although present in the house, is not available to you. You cannot communicate effectively; you cannot operate as a team. In your opinion, your partner is essentially absent.

How can you broach this problem and reach an amicable solution? Can you readjust your thinking around the issue to accommodate the other perspective?

The task here is to become more aware of the fact that there are always other ways of looking at an issue. Your own opinion and ideas matter enormously, and should be listened to and acknowledged. But the same goes for the other person.

How to React When You Feel Challenged by Your Partner's Behaviour or Attitude – The 8-Step Plan

1. Don't panic. This does not have to become a major crisis. Stay calm and give yourself time to think before reacting hastily and causing unnecessary friction.
2. Put the problem into perspective. How important is this issue to you and your happiness in this relationship?
3. Now examine your thinking on this issue. Where does it come from? Are you blindly following a belief system you were brought up with, or is this something about which you really do feel strongly?
4. What about your partner? Listen to their side of the story. Can you see what is so special about this issue?
5. You have two choices: either you accept your partner's thinking or behaviour or you try to reach a compromise. Which do you want to do?
6. Bear in mind the words of Buddhist monk Thích Nhất Hạnh, '*In true dialogue, both sides are willing to change.*' To what extent are you willing to change?
7. Discuss a compromise. What are you both willing to concede?
8. Agreeing to differ is fine. But each of you must be sure that the issue does not have a negative impact on your relationship.

Case Study

Let's look at the story of Amanda and Karl. Amanda is very outspoken on the matter of chewing gum. She considers it a really disgusting habit: antisocial, polluting, offensive. But Karl has always chewed gum. He cannot imagine a day without it. He says it relaxes him and has a relaxing effect on others in his company – except for Amanda, that is. And he does dispose of it properly: wrapping it in paper before binning it. But none of this changes Amanda's opinion.

So they make it the subject of a listening exercise. This time, as Amanda listens to Karl wax lyrical on the benefits of this disgusting goo, she finds herself for the first time realising just how much it means to him. Chewing gum is, for him, much more than that. It is happy childhood days hanging out with his mates; it is family jokes about who can chew a wad the longest. It is about feeling carefree and unstressed.

Amanda has never considered chewing gum as anything other than a blight on society. Now here it is presented with all the attributes of a wonder cure, a balm for sore nerves, almost a blessing. She swallows hard before feeding back what she has heard.

When Karl has listened to Amanda's opinion, he tries to see things from her perspective. He acknowledges that he has not until now appreciated the degree of annoyance and upset caused by his habit. He could cut it down, he concedes. But he cannot bear to hear Amanda demonise chewing gum to such an extent.

Fair point, Amanda agrees. Why does she react so radically to this rather harmless habit?

She thinks back over her childhood and immediately hears her mother go on and on about the appalling and cheap behaviour of chewers of gum. She even recalls her own discomfort at her mother's intolerance. Amanda did not like to hear her friends being criticised. But she still adopted her mother's attitude and has never chewed gum herself.

It transpires then, that the chewing of gum has become a vehicle for a different issue for both of them. For Karl it is a way of connecting with his happy past. For Amanda it is the transference of a set of values passed down from her mother. The total intolerance is more her mother's than Amanda's. Yet she has swallowed it whole and today is her first time to question her own prejudice.

The conclusion to this exercise is that the central issue has now diminished hugely in importance – it no longer bothers Amanda to the same extent if Karl chews gum. She sees her aversion as inherited. When she examines it objectively, she realises that gum is not as awful or as poisonous as she used to think. Interestingly, Karl has also begun to look at the chewing of gum for what it is. Now that he has articulated the reason for its importance in his life, he no longer needs gum to connect him to his past. He even admits that he has recently felt it is a rather childish habit. The other guys in the office don't chew gum. So he is thinking about giving it up.

SESSION ONE

Arrange a time to do this exercise together. As usual, make this dedicated time, free from other distractions. Think of an issue on which you both differ. Maybe it is screen time, or what one of you regards as an irrational dislike of something the other enjoys.

- Talk about it in a structured way, allowing each person five minutes to explain their point of view.
- Think about your own attitude. Could you change it somewhat by being more open-minded?
- Can you define why you are so intolerant around this issue? Explain it to your partner.
- Try to see things from your partner's perspective. Does that change your attitude more?
- Have you been taking this issue too seriously? Is there a funny side to all of this?
- What changes would you like to see in your partner's behaviour or reaction around your issue?
- Can each of you reach an understanding that will accommodate your differences?
- Can you agree to a trade-off – I'll accept this if you will agree to something else?

N.B. Watch out for what I call absolutism – refusing absolutely to even consider another perspective.

> Unless the issue is one of an attitude or behaviour that you feel is damaging to the relationship, be prepared to yield somewhat.

How to Handle an Argument

Conflict Causes Arguments

Conflict is a natural part of the human experience. It is neither wrong nor bad. The Oxford English Dictionary defines conflict as 'a state of opposition or hostilities; a fight or struggle; the clashing of opposed principles'. It is only to be expected that every couple will clash at times on certain issues. As with anger, it is how you handle conflict that matters.

Conflict is not necessarily something negative. It can highlight what is not working well in the relationship. Through conflict we can get an insight into our blind spot, that part of us that is seen by others but not by ourselves. So try looking at conflict as an opportunity to learn more about yourself.

However, some couples find conflict a real challenge. They say they have difficulty in discussing almost any issue without it escalating into an argument. And, as you know, once people begin to argue tempers get frayed and language becomes emotive, even abusive. Rational thinking goes out the window. This is when people say things they later regret. It is difficult to claw back what has been said in the heat of the moment. So the secret lies in learning to avoid uttering the wrong words or pressing the wrong buttons. By now you will be able to apply the techniques that you have learned in the programme so far. This should help to avoid such a scenario.

SESSION TWO

Despite our best efforts, there often remain certain core issues or sensitive topics to trigger the emotional response that leads to an argument. For this session, read through the issues outlined below and then devise your own list. Ask your partner to do the same.

See below some common causes of rows between couples with suggestions for resolution:

- *Behaviour: actions, inactions or habits of your partner that you find irritating.*
  - Address your irritation first. Try to identify the emotion that underlies your irritation or anger. Then tell your partner how the behaviour makes you feel.
- *Money: managing your finances can be a big source of stress in relationships.*
  - Be honest and open with one another. Work towards joint decision-making.
- *Parenting: whose parenting style prevails?*
  - Avoid taking opposing stances: good cop v bad cop; lenient v strict. Children quickly learn to play one parent off against the other. Instead, discuss your parenting options away from the children. Aim to agree on a joint approach as much as possible.
- *Misunderstandings: poor communication can cause unnecessary friction.*
  - Become more conscious of your language when giving a message. If you are receiving the message, listen carefully and ask for clarification if it is needed.

What are your common causes of rows? Jot them down. How could each of you handle sensitive issues differently in the future? Talk about it.

Argument Patterns – Which Is Yours?

From my experience of working with couples, it seems to me that arguments usually follow one of three patterns:

1. *Circular* – the circle speaks for itself. Meet Charlie and Anne. Anne starts off with a complaint: Charlie has

forgotten to put out the bins. Charlie gets annoyed – the bins were put out on time last week, yet Anne gave him no credit for that. That in turn annoys Anne – does Charlie not realise how much work she does around the house that goes unnoticed? And this is not the first time she has had to remind him about the bins.

'*That's exactly the point*', Charlie argues. '*All you ever do is complain about those wretched bins. Why not put them out yourself since you are so good at remembering?*'

Tension is rising fast now. Anne feels not just angry but hurt as well. So she gives as good as she gets:

'*I always knew you were a lazy so-and-so.*'

Round and round they go. Insults mount up; tempers get frayed. Both Charlie and Anne realise that they have been down this road many times before. There is no resolution regarding the bins.

2. *Labyrinthine* – were you ever unable to remember how a row started? Enter Charlie and Anne stage left. Bin day has passed and the full bin still sits in the side passage. Anne complains to Charlie. Charlie gets angry. He is tired of being constantly under attack as he sees it.

'*Look who's talking*', he says. '*What about you losing the car keys last week?*'

'*What has that to do with the bins? But if you want to talk about forgetfulness, who forgot his passport last summer? We could have lost a few days of our holidays. I was never so stressed in all my life.*'

Charlie is resourceful. He is not going to have more accusations levelled at him than he can throw at Anne. So off they go down one blind alley after another. By the time they run out of energy or accusations, they have forgotten about the bins.

3. *Linear* – Charlie has forgotten to put out the bins yet again. Anne is frustrated. What can she say that will change this all-too-familiar situation? When Charlie comes home she says nothing for a while. She hopes that he will notice the

full bin and realise his mistake. But that does not happen. Later that evening, when the children are in bed, Anne broaches the subject:

'Charlie, the food bin was not emptied today. You remembered to put out the green bin last week which was great. What can we do that will help you remember bin day every week?'

'Sorry about that. As you say, I got it right last week. Maybe I could set a reminder on my phone.'

'That's a great idea. And we can mark it on the notice board in the kitchen.'

'Now there's no need to overdo it. Let's first see how the reminder works.'

As you can see, this is more a discussion than an argument. Why? Charlie and Anne both helped prevent it from developing into a full-blown row. Anne remained calm and did not make Charlie feel under attack. For his part, Charlie accepted his responsibility and even apologised. So their conversation followed a logical progression from start to resolution.

SESSION THREE

When Conflict Occurs: Establishing the Ground Rules

This is a joint session with your partner. Choose a time when you are both feeling calm and free from conflict.

As we have already established, it is vital to keep the channels of communication open no matter what the issue is. If rows and arguments tend to escalate out of control, you and your partner need to set down some ground rules. This is your task in Session Three. In your notebook write out your agreed list of dos and don'ts. Here are some suggestions to start with:

- No shouting
- No verbal abuse
- Each person has the right to be heard without interruption
- Add your own ground rules as you see fit; it may be to disallow some negative behaviour which you or your partner tend to use during an argument

Now study the points below and discuss them with your partner. The more you think about them, the more you will be able to put them into practice.

The Keys to Handling Confrontation Effectively

- Establish the ground rules in advance.
- Keep the noise level down. Once people start shouting at each other, they are no longer rational. Emotions run high and soon things are being said which are later regretted.
- Take a few deep breaths before engaging. This will reduce the stress levels.
- Think before you retort. A moment's thought here can avoid things escalating out of control.
- Assess the situation. Where does this issue fit on a scale of 1–10? Is this really worth all your negative energy?
- Remember to use your WITT – see Step Three. Choose your words and the information you want to convey, time your discussion well and watch your tone.
- Allow your partner have their say. Can you truly hear what is being said? See the listening exercise in Stage Four.
- If you have initiated this row, try to identify your motivation. Is your underlying interest in establishing fairness, agreeing on a safety issue or ensuring mutual respect? Or is this a tit-for-tat exercise?
- Focus on feelings – see Step Five. Name your own feelings and observe those of your partner. If they

are not named, suggest them: *'So you must have felt quite confused/angry/hurt ...'*. This helps each of you understand why the other is upset.

- Even if your partner is not adhering to the rules, show by example. There is nothing more effective than a gentle but firm response to take down the anger levels.
- In conflict, each partner must acknowledge and accept their role. By doing that, you are less likely to become overly emotional. You can each contribute to a resolution.
- Don't ever tolerate being bullied. Name it. Even if hurtful remarks are being delivered with a smile, they are not acceptable. *'I was only joking'* is no excuse if the other person feels insulted.
- Focus on *what* is right, not on *who* is right. Arguments should not be about winning or losing. It is not a competition. Never forget that you are a team.
- Contain your conflict. The argument you have with your partner is between the two of you.
- Even you can get it wrong sometimes. Be prepared to say sorry. It can work wonders.

ONGOING EXERCISE

How to Avoid Common Pitfalls When Having an Argument

- Refuse to use sarcasm or cutting comments. These do not show your intelligence or wit. They just indicate that you are feeling insecure.
- Don't resort to the blame game, it only exacerbates the tension. By dumping all the responsibility onto your partner, you exonerate the only person you can change – yourself.
- Avoid as far as possible involving friends or extended family to try to get them on your side. Above all,

don't resort to publicising your differences on social media. That increases the possibility of lasting damage.
- Keep your emotions in check. Sometimes couples articulate their worst fears as a challenge to the other. Matters can soon get dramatic and out of hand. Read the case study below.

Case Study

I recall a young wife who had low self-esteem. She felt so insecure that she could not tolerate her husband looking at other women. She was constantly on high alert, watching out for him watching them. Her husband felt confused and saddened. Surely he could look at anyone they saw when they were out? Surely she trusted him? He tried to reassure her. But his wife was adamant that he should look at no other woman.

'So why don't you go off with her?' she'd taunt whenever she spotted a possible rival. 'You obviously like her more than me.'

One day, years later, that is exactly what happened. He did go off with another woman, who in fact was not as physically attractive as his wife. The continued goading had become intolerable for him. He wanted a relationship based on trust and mutual respect. The young wife had managed to make her worst fears come true.

Getting It All Together

I hope that by now you have both been practising the 8-step plan for challenging your partner's behaviour or attitude as set out earlier in this chapter. You will find that it is also a great tool when handling an argument. Try using it next time you and your partner disagree. You are bound to have different outlooks and attitudes on certain issues. In fact, you should feel comfortable to disagree with your partner. The key to handling these disagreements successfully is quite simple:

- Keep cool – it is only natural that you and your partner will disagree at times.
- Don't take it as a personal insult that your partner does not always share your outlook.
- Respect your partner's right to hold their own opinion.
- A difference of opinion need not develop into a row.
- Practise having a discussion on issues where you disagree. A good lively discussion can be fun.

See how easy life becomes when you don't have constant rows.

Concluding an Argument

It is most important that an argument is ended properly.

- Each party should feel they have been heard. For some couples this is a really satisfying moment. Thank your partner for hearing you out.
- Even if your opinions still differ, respect the other person's view.
- If applicable, agree on a resolution.
- If you feel the argument went off course, talk about it. *'Next time this situation arises, how could we handle it better?'*

Feedback

Keep practising your new techniques. It takes a while for them to become automatic. When the next disagreement occurs, remind each other of how you are going to handle the situation. Repeat the steps outlined in this chapter.

Remember too that these are life skills that you can apply to many situations of disagreement: with your children or with work colleagues. Once you stay calm and reasonable, your adversary will adjust accordingly. You will soon find that your life in general has become much more agreeable.

Step Seven

DOWNTIME TOGETHER – KEEP ON DATING

Step Seven helps you and your partner put the fun back into your relationship. It encourages you to take a look at how you organise and prioritise your life. By the end of this step, you and your spouse should be back in centre stage position, where you belong.

One of the most powerful realisations I have had in my years in counselling is that there are no parallel lines in a relationship. Every day you and your partner either grow closer together or drift further apart. You may think that this idea makes no sense – maybe in recent weeks you have not had much time to talk intimately to one another, but neither have you had any rows. You are not aware of any distance between you. But my experience has shown that this lack of connection takes its toll, however slight. It is only when you reconnect that you realise how much you have to catch up on.

The Three T's Challenge

To ensure that you and your spouse are connecting effectively, do a Three T's check-up from time to time.

- *Time together* – despite all the other demands on your time, do you both make dedicated, real time to be there for each other?
- *Talking* – this means talking about you two, not about children, household management or finance.

- *Touching* – do you make an effort to be in touch and then to stay in touch with one another? Try to connect in subtle ways – a kiss, a hug, a touch in passing.

Restoring the Situation

Our daily lives affect the way we think and react. Small but significant things happen which, if left untold, may be forgotten. If you and your partner make time to communicate for just a few minutes at the end of each day, there is little chance of you drifting too far apart.

There is something special about a night out together. No children, no IT, no distractions. Choose a restaurant where you both feel comfortable. Ask for a window or wall table where you will be out of the main restaurant traffic. Dress up a bit – remember how you used to make sure you looked well when you were first dating? Well, the idea here is to make this the first of regular date nights from now on.

Yes. All couples need to go out together as regularly as possible – if not every week, then at least every two weeks. Make date night part of your routine. Once it is established you will find you look forward to it more and more.

If you feel that you can't afford to go out so often then go for a less expensive option – a walk, a movie, a cup of coffee. The important thing is that it is just the two of you and that you have a relaxing time.

When did you two last sit down to a candlelit meal together in a relaxed atmosphere? You can't remember? The trouble is that with everything else in your lives so scheduled and demanding, you probably have not factored in time for the most important person in your life – your partner.

'*How has this happened to us? Where is the happy couple who were so deeply in love and who always had time for each other?*'

The interesting word here is HAD. The thing is, you always had time for each other because you MADE time for each other.

A busy lifestyle places huge demands on your time. But when you look back you realise that in the early days of your relationship you were determined to make time for your partner, no matter how busy you were.

SESSION ONE

Your Special Story

So what is the difference today? Where are those two people who smile at you from the photo on the mantelpiece? Have you lost touch with that couple so happy and in love? They are right here still but somewhat smothered underneath layers of work, responsibilities and busyness.

It may take a while to peel off those layers, but you know that a large part of each of you is still the same today as you were then. Sit down together and take another look at the photo. Recount the story of when you first met. What attracted you to one another? What did you like most about each other? If you have children, they will love this – they relish hearing your story again and again. It gives them an insight into you as young adults, lovers and best friends, not just as their parents.

Remember your first date? Talk about it. Recall your feelings then. Have you any funny memories of when things went wrong? There is something special about retelling your own story and reliving those feelings. All you have to do now is organise the next stage of your story. Don't wait for all those wonderful feelings to simply magic themselves back. Remember that actions generate feelings. Doing something romantic makes you feel romantic.

By the end of this session you will hopefully feel energised by those happy memories. Now resolve to add an extra act of kindness to your partner into your daily routine.

The Set Up

I trust that by now you are convinced of the importance of regular, relaxed time together. This should be two to three hours per week, just the two of you – no others allowed – away from all distractions. If possible, try to go out together for a meal, a drink, a walk, a talk, or a combination. Walking is good but, because you are not facing one another, it is not ideal for an intimate discussion. So try to factor in some face-to-face time.

The undoubted attractions of eating out speak for themselves – no work, no mobiles (be sure they're switched off), no screens – just the two of you in, hopefully, a relaxed setting. Choose a venue where you both feel comfortable. Make it a date. Make it once a week, adjusting the activity to suit your situation. Agree on your date day. If other commitments interfere, re-schedule date night so that you still have your weekly time together. Take turns in organising the event.

Soon you will find that your time together has become a beacon, a source of comfort when you feel under pressure. Having something to look forward to is a most effective balm during the week, soothing bad temper or stress, enabling you to perform better at your work.

When you are out together, be sure to spend time talking about yourselves:

- How does each of you feel?
- How has the week been?
- Were there any issues that arose at work or at home which you would like to discuss?
- Have you any stories from the week that you have not had time to share?
- Is your partner looking well? If yes, say so. Everyone enjoys a compliment. If not, is something causing stress?
- Express appreciation for something that your partner did during the week.
- Talk about your fears or anxieties. It can make you feel less stressed. Once expressed, these worries lose the dread factor

– especially when seen through the eyes of another. You may even get to laugh at yourself for being too fearful.
- Tell your partner of little actions that make you feel special, excited: '*I love it when you ...*'.
- Enjoy one another. Life together is, after all, meant to be fun.

Once you have developed the habit of dating again, you will find that you store up a bank of little things that happen during the week, to share with your partner on your night out.

ONGOING EXERCISE

This assignment is easy. You must make it an automatic part of your lives together. Just make sure you do each of the following from now on:

- Start dating again. Assign one evening each week for you as a couple. Do whatever it takes to create a time and space for you two alone. Arrange for a babysitter. Try to get out of the house – go for a walk, go for a drink, go for a meal. If you go to the theatre or cinema, factor in some time to chat – maybe over a cup of coffee afterwards.
- Try not to cancel your date night. If other engagements encroach, re-schedule it for another day that week.
- Agree in advance – the conversation on date night must not be totally dominated by your children or other family members. Remember, this is your time to talk to each other about each other. That is what happened when you were first dating. Let your partner know what has been going on for you in the past week: your worries, your achievements, some silly events which you might not normally have time to talk about.
- Dress up a bit for your night out together – remember, you're going on a date.

- This must be a screen-free event – no sneaky glances at your Facebook page.

Many couples have told me that this one adjustment to their schedules has had a hugely positive impact on their lives.

'We have fallen in love all over again', one couple wrote. *'We had become so used to focusing on our children and our work, that we no longer saw each other as boyfriend and girlfriend. Now the spark is back in our lives.'*

Trouble-Shooting Guide

- *I am still waiting for my partner to organise our date night* – Stop waiting. If you want to go out together, why don't you organise it? How much organisation does it take? A phone call or two? It will be worth the effort. Do you apportion responsibility for every element of your lives together, afraid that you might do more than your fair share?
- *I've organised the last two date nights – now it's up to my partner.* Keep the bigger picture in mind. Date night is too important to flounder because of a tit-for-tat mentality. What does your partner say? Discuss it before your next night out.
- *We've nothing to say to each other anymore.* Sounds like you have got out of the habit of relaxing together. Try drawing on your bank of shared memories. Recall some fun times from your dating days. Watch a favourite movie together. Then talk about it.
- *There's no point in going out together – we'll only end up having a row.* That is why date night comes at this stage of the programme. First you need to work on your communication skills. Try the listening exercise in Step Four and the section on how to handle an argument in Step Six. Once you learn how to listen to one another you will find

that you speak to one another with greater respect and patience.

- *We simply can't afford to go out on a date night, certainly not once a week.* What do you enjoy doing together that does not cost too much? You can always have an early meal at home and then go out just for a drink. Or try date night at home. The same rules apply – commitment to a specific time, IT free, just the two of you. Get a takeaway or prepare an easy meal; put on your favourite music; use the good plates and glassware. And don't forget to light some candles.

- *I just don't feel like going out on a date with my partner.* Feeling out of love with your partner is not an uncommon occurrence in most long-term relationships. The question is, what do you do about it? You can either cling to that position and remain stubbornly negative and perhaps self-pitying, or you can take action to bring about a change. Try doing a little act of kindness for your partner each day for the next week. Perhaps they won't even notice at first. But don't give up. Doing something kind for your partner will make you feel better about yourself and will eventually bring about a change in the atmosphere between you.

- *We don't have a babysitter.* Don't worry. Rise to the challenge. How about coming to an arrangement with friends: one of you babysits their children on Friday nights; they return the favour on Saturday nights. Meantime, start looking in earnest for a babysitter – it's good to have a Plan B.

- *My partner tends to drink too much when we go out.* Two points here – firstly, discuss your thoughts on this with your partner. Do they feel the need for professional help? What are your thoughts and fears on the issue? Encourage your partner to seek professional help if you think it is required. Secondly, choose an alcohol-free zone for your date nights. Cafes can provide a quiet haven as well as good food. Or, if you go to a restaurant, agree beforehand that you will not order alcohol.

- *A night out sounds great but we are too busy.* So what does that say about the importance of your relationship in your lives? Yes, some stages of our lives are much busier than others, but stop and think for a moment. Write down a list of all the things that take up your time. Then write a list of the priorities in your life. Where does your relationship rank? How much would a night out with your partner cost? What is the cost of ignoring your relationship with the one you love?

- *We went out on a date night but it was a disaster!* Don't expect everything to work out brilliantly on the first try. Think about it – you were able to enjoy dating your partner in the past. It is not that you have lost the ability to enjoy yourselves together. It's just that you need practice before you get things right. Read over the guidelines again. Choose another venue where you will both feel comfortable. Laugh about the disaster night – then plan the next night out together.

Still Reluctant to Commit to Date Nights?

If you are still reluctant to commit to regular date nights, it is good to pause and consider. What is the thinking behind this resistance? Perhaps your discomfort comes from a feeling that this is extravagance, that you don't deserve to be treated well or that you are fundamentally unlovable.

Feeling unlovable, as opposed to feeling unloved, is an indication of low self-esteem. This feeling of unworthiness or even shame can be addressed by looking at how you look at yourself. Here are some thoughts to help change a negative self-image:

- You are only as attractive as you feel you deserve to be. So allow yourself to accept positive messages from your partner.
- The more you give to others the more your capacity to love grows. Thinking of others in a loving way helps open your heart to receiving love.

- Love starts with accepting the self – see Stage One of the programme. Deepak Chopra tells us, '*Love is Spirit; Spirit is the self.*'
- If you are still clinging to your belief that you are unlovable, tell yourself that it is you and you alone who places this obstacle in the way of love. Maybe your negative thoughts are based on fears created by a memory. The challenge now is to look beyond those negative experiences in the past. Can you allow yourself to move on?
- I leave the final thought here to Deepak Chopra: '*if you can radiate simple unaffected humanity, you will be immensely lovable.*'

Ready for date night now? Relax, lighten up and go for it!

Feedback

Allow yourselves time to get into the swing of date nights. There can be teething problems initially – choosing the wrong venue, expecting too much too soon or one of you being less enthusiastic than the other. So wait until you have gone on at least four date nights before assessing the situation. Check in with one another – what changes would make it more fun for you both?

Avoid the pitfall of feeling guilty about spending money on yourselves. This can happen especially when you have young children. Just remember that by investing in your relationship with your partner, you are creating a happier home environment. This in turn will benefit your children much more than you may realise.

Keep up your date nights. Always have the next one planned. Remember that the anticipation of that next oasis of calm and togetherness can help you through the tough days.

Step Eight

SEX AND OUR ATTITUDE TO IT

When you consider the preoccupation with sex in the media and our constant exposure to sex and sexuality, it is surprising to note that in fact the very same problems with intimacy in relationships that have always been there are still around for couples today. Why is this? It is because in many societies and cultures we have not yet managed to accept our sexual side as an intrinsic part of being human. We put our sexual selves into a separate compartment, not to be opened except in cases of emergency. Talk of sex and sexuality makes us uncomfortable. We either make it the subject of lewd jokes or we pretend that it does not exist.

So what happens? We grow up learning how to build a healthy relationship with our other appetites or needs – for food, comfort, knowledge, shelter and companionship. But we often fail to get to know or to come to terms with our sexual needs. This can mean that we are poorly equipped to form a meaningful intimate relationship. But in Step Eight I think that you will find the information and encouragement to enable you to address any sexual issues with your partner.

Step Eight helps you look at the story of your sexual development. In this chapter we also explore the most common complaints couples have in relation to their sex life. You will see that if you have a problem in relation to sex you are not alone. But, more importantly, you will learn how to deal successfully with your sexual issues.

The Beauty of Sexual Intimacy

When two people commit to one another in marriage, they express a desire to share their lives intimately. The ultimate act of intimacy is sexual union – the two become one.

The beauty of sexual intimacy is difficult to describe in words. It is a profound connection that bonds the couple, allowing them to express their deepest desires to one another, binding them together in love. Sexual intimacy is about gentleness, about caring, about being vulnerable together, about sharing our bare selves. It is also about having fun together, getting to know each other's bodies, exploring pleasure zones, de-stressing. A healthy sex life can go a long way towards making a relationship work. But, because it is so intimate, sexual intimacy is often the first casualty when relationship problems occur.

Sexual Development

The messages you received about sex as a child have probably influenced the way you think of your sexual self today. Can you recall when you first became aware of yourself as a sexual being? Was it as you entered adolescence or was it earlier?

From the moment of birth, we instinctively seek the comfort of human contact – a newborn baby searches for that soothing touch. Children look to their parents for protection and affection to help them thrive. As children become adolescents a type of decoupling takes place. The onset of adolescence is signalled by physical changes that are primarily sexual. The young adult body develops the capability to procreate. Alongside these physical changes there is a drive to establish their own identity and autonomy. Parents may become a source of embarrassment at this time.

While moving away somewhat from parental dependence, teenagers still want to belong, still want a connection. So they tend to gravitate more towards their peers. But do their peers know any more about sexuality than themselves? It is no wonder that, for many, the teenage years can be confusing and complex. There is the excitement of becoming aware of the physical changes of sexual development. But this excitement can be mixed with fear caused by ignorance or misinformation. There is also an element of embarrassment as adolescents try to adjust to their new and developing selves. This may result in lots of tittering and giggling. If the embarrassment is more acute, the teenager may become quite withdrawn and feel awkward socially.

Pressure from their peers can exacerbate the situation. The confused teenager cannot distinguish between truth and bragging. Hormonal changes contribute to the confusion, producing starkly contrasting moods. One minute the teenager wants to be a child, the next they want to flee the nest. This is where good family support really matters.

Masturbation is usually discovered during adolescence. This is a normal rite of passage, part of the journey of self-discovery. Self-pleasuring helps you get comfortable with your own body. Masturbation is usually carried out in private, so there is an element of secrecy involved. This sometimes leads to feelings of guilt. It is important that masturbation is accepted and acknowledged as a normal part of sexual development. It is a source of comfort, a form of self-soothing, replacing the comforts of childhood. But an over-dependence on masturbation can be unhealthy. If it is combined with looking at pornographic images, there is a potential for real and long-term damage.

What are your memories of your developing years? Now that you have a life partner it is good to share your memories with one another.

Sex and Us

Sex forms an intrinsic part of a couple's relationship. It is a basic and essential ingredient. The importance of sexual intimacy should not be underestimated. After all, if the sexual part of your relationship is removed you might as well be siblings or simply friends sharing accommodation.

We are hard-wired to be sexual beings. We must have sex if we are to continue the human race. Sex is a survival imperative. The attraction you felt for one another from the start of your relationship was primarily sexually driven. You have an inbuilt desire to choose a partner with whom you feel sexually comfortable. If you want to have children you also choose a partner whom you consider suitable as a parent for your future children.

It is always dangerous to make generalisations. Yet the prevailing truth regarding sex and our attitude to it is this:

A man falls in love because of the way he feels when he is with a woman. He needs sexual fulfilment in order to respond emotionally. To a man sex is a most meaningful way of expressing emotion. It makes a man feel fulfilled, more of a man.

A woman first needs emotional fulfilment before she responds sexually. She needs to feel loved and appreciated, that her man cares about her, before she is interested in engaging in sex.

How do you respond to these statements? Discuss them with your partner. Do you think there is any truth in them for you? As the male partner do you tend to have a more urgent drive to have sex and to climax than your wife? As the female are you slower to achieve arousal and in need of longer foreplay? Are there changes that you would like to see in the pattern of your lovemaking?

Common Myths about Sex

- *Real men are always ready for sex* – just think of how much pressure this puts on men. The sexual drive among men varies hugely, just as it does among women. If a woman buys into this myth she may make teasing or undermining comments about her husband's sexual prowess. As a result, her partner could develop performance anxiety leading to sexual dysfunction. But confidence can be restored with gentle encouragement and support.
- *Good girls don't express sexual desires* – despite the supposed liberation of women, this myth still holds sway in many cultures. In fact, it is so engrained in our thinking that it is often reflected in language. Take the English language as an example. If a man expresses sexual desires

he is called 'a stud', 'a cool guy', 'Don Juan' or 'Valentino', or 'he's cock of the walk'. All positive labels that are worn with pride. But for the sexually desirous female the language is different. She is known as 'a slut', 'a slapper' or 'a whore', or 'she's easy got' and 'she has a want'. Not exactly flattering terms I think you would agree. The message is clear – good girls with self-respect should not express sexual desire.

The result is that some women regard sex as something to be endured, necessary for procreation only. Once they have had their children, they lose interest in sexual activity. This attitude can undermine the sacred bond and deep connection of intimacy that is the foundation stone of marriage.

- *If you don't use it you lose it* – this myth probably originates in the teenage years. Because it is done in secret, masturbation is frequently rushed. There is an urgency to progress to climax before being discovered. Unless informed otherwise, many men bring this pattern of urgency into their relationship. What they don't realise is that they can lose an erection and regain it several times before reaching ejaculation.

  This myth can also carry some truth when applied to getting out of practice in any skill. When sexual intercourse becomes very infrequent, when a couple falls out of the habit of making love, it can be a challenge to get back in touch again. See the trouble-shooting guide below.

- *A woman's role is to satisfy a man* – while most people will reject this notion as ridiculous, it can still have an insidious hold at a subconscious level. A woman who buys into this myth will ignore her own sexual needs, focusing solely on her sexual partner. This in time leads her to lose interest until she ends up playing a passive role in lovemaking. A man who accepts this myth will ignore his wife's sexual needs. In time, lovemaking will become less exciting and more functional for both. But when a man is sensitive to the fluctuations of his wife's levels of desire, when he knows that desire peaks with fertility, then both parties will be more in tune with one another when making love.

- *All lovemaking should end in intercourse* – the problem with this myth is that it can have a really negative effect on your sexual relationship. If every expression of intimacy from a kiss to a touch is seen as a precursor to sexual intercourse, there may be trouble brewing. Intimacy has now become the first stage on the road that, in the eyes of one partner at least, leads inevitably to penetrative sex. So the response to any show of affection can become negative.

  Of course, intimacy is an intrinsic and essential part of lovemaking leading to sexual intercourse. But its role should be much broader than that. When intercourse is not possible for health or other reasons, or when one partner is unwilling to have intercourse, it is really important to stay feeling close to one another. Kissing, cuddling and touching should be part of your everyday lives. Use intimacy to say '*I love you*', '*I am sensitive to what you're feeling right now*', '*I'm here for you*'. Avoid interpreting any show of intimacy as an unspoken demand for or promise to have intercourse.

- *Sex should always be spontaneous* – remember the good old days when you seemed to have sex at the drop of a hat? Perhaps that was back in the days before having children and a mortgage. But look again – were things really so spontaneous when you were newly-weds? Did you not rush home after work each day just to be together? Did you not organise date nights at the weekends? Maybe it was easier to have sex in those early days, but was there not usually some forward planning involved?

  No doubt you schedule to satisfy your other needs – times to eat, sleep, exercise and work are all factored into your timetable. So is it not a good idea to create space for your sex life as well?

- *If my partner really loved me then they would know how I feel about our sex life* – surely this is an unfair expectation. How is your partner to know how you feel if you are unwilling to articulate your wishes? Are you relying on your partner to fulfil their side of a psychological contract known only to you? These unilateral contracts are based on your image or expectation of your partner, e.g. *'to truly love someone is to know how they feel without having to be told'*. Or *'my partner knows that I'm uncomfortable talking about sex, so they should just know what I think without my having to say it'*.

Maybe it is time to stop wishing, waiting and wanting. Maybe it is time to talk frankly and openly to one another.

Less Frequent Sex

If you and your spouse have previously enjoyed what you consider to be a good sexual relationship, it can come as a shock if one of you becomes increasingly reluctant to make love. This unease around lovemaking may be subtle enough at first. There are valid excuses initially. But just when you feel that things should be back on track, there are more excuses. Once they have been exhausted, things still do not pick up. Lovemaking has been relegated to the back burner. You now realise that there is more to this than you first appreciated.

You need to talk. But perhaps you and your partner have never had a frank discussion about your lovemaking. Maybe one or both of you feel awkward about it. Maybe you are afraid of saying what you really feel in case you hurt your partner's feelings. Here are some of the most common causes of less frequent sex in couples I have dealt with:

- *The initial excitement has worn off* – this is an indication of the couple's idea of what sex is all about. Perhaps they think it is only about the adrenalin rush of the infatuation stage of a relationship. In that case it is understandable that once the getting-to-know-you phase has passed, sex will lose its meaning. They will want to move on to a new sexual partner.

   But once a couple sees sex as the way to form a deep and lasting connection, they realise that the initial excitement is indeed just the first phase of their relationship. And there will be lots of exciting and fulfilling times ahead, while they get to know one another more intimately and deeply in the course of a long and happy relationship.

- *Too preoccupied or busy at work* – this may apply to one or both partners, when work plays too big a role in their lives. But the consequences are usually first felt by one partner. It is important to recognise the fallout before it takes too big a toll on the relationship. Make time to be intimate. Put yourselves back in your rightful position centre stage.
- *Having a baby* – the arrival of your baby is a momentous event. The joy, the excitement, the sleepless nights, the worry lest anything go wrong – everything is in the mix. Mothers can feel very fulfilled and satisfied from bonding with baby. Fathers may feel excluded, overlooked or neglected.

  Add to this the challenge to mothers, especially first-time mums, of adjusting to their postnatal selves. Some new mums feel uncomfortable with their bodies, thinking that they are no longer sexually attractive. Others feel so maternal that they no longer experience a need for sexual intimacy. This stage varies in length but can continue for several months after childbirth.

  So what's to be done? Keep talking, keep touching, keep making time, however short, to be together. Keep supporting one another – let your partner know that you're there to help; try to understand what they are feeling. And enjoy this great adventure of parenthood together.
- *Sickness or depression* – a prolonged bout of sickness or depression can have a devastating effect on any relationship. For married couples it is a big challenge. Your partner, your teammate, your best buddy is suddenly at a remove. Their pain and suffering become your own. You want to be there for them, you want to make it all better, but you may feel powerless. Because sickness and depression are beyond your control.

  But the good news is that there is much you can do to help your partner. You can stay calm and supportive; you can keep in touch, literally touching, for the sense of touch is particularly healing. You can let your partner know that you are still teammates. And you can give them hope – that this dark phase will pass and there is a chink of light on the horizon.

- *Feeling less sexual or sexually attractive* – once you have decided on a negative self-image, your partner is almost powerless to change your mind. You probably also filter out any positive messages from others, telling yourself that they are just trying to cheer you up; that they don't really mean it. If this is the case, you are going to have to do the work yourself – it is up to you to allow yourself some positivity. Start with a self-focus exercise – see Step One. As you become more accepting of yourself, allow thoughts of sex back onto your mental agenda. Think back to when you felt sexy and good about yourself. If you don't have a memory bank to draw on, start imagining what feeling really sexy would be like.

- *Constantly tired* – everyone feels tired at times. But chronic tiredness needs to be addressed. Are you working too hard? If so, cut back on your hours. Remember to prioritise your relationship. Do you think you may be sick? Get a health check. Or has saying you're tired become your default position at the prospect of making love with your partner? Maybe some elements of all three scenarios ring true for you. Whatever the reasons, take stock and see what you can do to change the impasse. Firstly, talk about it – how does your partner feel? What would you both like to see happen? Try going to bed earlier and together.

- *Loss of libido and loss of interest* – this can be a chicken and egg situation, one begets the other. Losing your libido, for whatever reason, can dent your confidence. The fear of failing to achieve arousal or climax puts you off having sex. The more you evade sexual activity, the more you lose interest. In order to avoid going down this negative spiral, when you are challenged with loss of libido or loss of interest, try to keep intimacy alive. Be patient with yourself and each other. Encourage one another. Your patience, understanding and determination will make this phase pass.

- *I'm fine, don't worry about me* – what is the message here? That I don't count, that I am unimportant, that our sex life is all about your needs and not mine? Marriage is about caring, about sharing, about helping the other feel valued and special. So is sex. Both of you matter. Don't settle for one partner saying their needs don't count. If one of you disengages, both of you lose out. Sex can then become merely functional as you are deprived of the comfort and closeness that intimacy brings.

Poor Sexual Patterns and What to Do to Change Them

Think about your behaviour and attitude towards sex.

- *Has your sex life become very predictable over time?*
  - Try making it unpredictable once in a while.
- *Does one spouse always initiate sex?*
  - Why not change the pattern here and surprise your partner?
- *Have you developed roles of pursuer v withdrawer in your sex life?*
  - What about changing roles?
- *What is your attitude to sex? Are you conservative or adventurous? Are you resistant to new ideas?*
  - Before you close your mind, open it.

How important is your sex life to you? How does your partner feel? If you feel that sex is not important, think again. Your sexual relationship with your partner is so precious. Allow it to develop, evolve and deepen. Then you will both enjoy the ever-changing, ever-deepening contentment and connection that intimacy brings.

Now it is time to take a look at your sex life and your attitude to it. This requires a bit of digging back into your childhood.

SESSION ONE

Work your way through the following questions on your own. Write your answers in your notebook. Ask your partner to do the same.

- When and from whom did you first learn about sex?
- Was sex talked about openly at home or was it never mentioned?
- What was the message about sex that you received from your parents?
- When you hear the word 'sex' now, what is your immediate reaction: embarrassment, excitement, anxiety, curiosity ...? Think about this.
- Are you happy with your reaction or do you find it rather childish? If you are uncomfortable, try saying the word aloud a few times. There is no great mystique to it really.
- Think again about the word 'sex' – what thoughts or sensations spring to mind? Write down some key words. Spend at least five minutes exploring your thoughts. Read over what you have written. Underline any feeling words, either positive or negative.
- Are you comfortable talking to your partner about your sex life?
- Have you and your partner enjoyed really good sex in the past?
- How do you rate your sex life at the moment?
- If your sex life has disimproved, what do you think are the contributing factors?
- How often do you and your partner make love these days? How often would you like to make love?
- How often are you playful together – kissing, cuddling, touching, teasing?
- Do you ever use sex as a bargaining tool in your relationship?
- Write down three situations that turn you on sexually.
- If you could add one ingredient to sex with your partner on an ongoing basis, what would it be?
- If you were to talk to your partner about how you would like to be pleasured, what would you say?
- If you could choose any setting for romantic, passionate, fulfilling sex with your partner, what would you opt for? Don't be modest here: forget about practicalities and costs – the sky's the limit.

- So, what did you come up with? Which elements of the scenario appeal to you most? Could you replicate some or all of this scenario here and now? How about it? How do you think your partner would react? Find out.

SESSION TWO

This is a joint session with your partner. When did you and your partner last have a frank discussion about sex? How comfortable were you?

Even more than in any other area in a relationship, talking about your sex life is most effective when certain ground rules are established between you. Our sexual needs, patterns and desires are so intimate and personal that we can become overly sensitive and defensive.

Ground Rules and Guidelines

- Choose a good time to talk about your sex life. You both need to feel as relaxed as possible.
- Promise to respect each other's thoughts or desires.
- Open the discussion as a listening exercise (see Step Four) – one speaks, the other listens, etc. Remember, in feedback, avoid giving your reaction – just report what you have heard. There will be time later for you to express your own thoughts on the subject.
- Agree to keep this confidential. This can be a real help if your partner feels uncomfortable talking about sex.
- Agree not to take suggestions for change as a personal slight. Be open to what your partner says. Some people choose to avoid any discussion of sex with their partner altogether in case they take offence. This is a shame. If you were aware that your partner would dearly love a change in your

lovemaking, you would probably be happy to make that change.

- You too may have secret desires that you have never articulated. Now is the time to do so. Forget the shyness – after all, what have you got to lose?

- If your partner lacks interest in sex, this usually indicates that the lovemaking pattern you use is not meeting their needs. In other words, they are not getting sufficient pleasure from lovemaking. So ask your partner to teach you how to improve as a lover.

- If either of you feels that there is a real sexual dysfunction, agree to seek professional help. For a man, the problem may be related to loss of libido or difficulty achieving and/or retaining an erection. For a woman it could be painful intercourse or an aversion to sex.

- But remember that many times a couple can resolve these issues themselves simply by being very attentive to what their partner is saying. Once each feels heard, it can make lovemaking more relaxed. So work on it.

Don't forget, making love should be fun. Be prepared to laugh when things go wrong. It is not the end of the world. After all, you have a whole lifetime ahead of you to get it right.

Trouble-Shooting Guide

When Sex Has Lost Its Meaning or When There Is No Sex

So, you can't remember when you last made love, or you can't remember when you last enjoyed making love? Address the problem:

- *We used to have a good sex life but that has all died.* Recall your happy sexual experiences together. What made it fun? Where were you? What did you feel? What did you do to one another then? What could you do now to re-create those feelings, that atmosphere? Set the scene in your bedroom. A warm, tidy room, clean sheets, mood music, soft lighting and sexy attire can help bring back the spark and the fun.

- *I have never enjoyed sex with my partner.* Have you enjoyed sex with others? If so, recall your experiences. What are your triggers for feeling sexually aroused? Can you recreate them? What would you like to see happening now? Tell your partner about the changes you would like to see in your lovemaking.

- *I have never enjoyed sex.* What do you really think about the sexual act? Do you avoid thinking about it? Our sexual side is a very valid and vital part of each human being. Value your sexual self. Have you ever explored your own sexual needs? Have you ever masturbated? Remember, this is a natural part of the maturing process. It helps you get to know your own body. Once you are comfortable with your body you can then allow your partner to pleasure it too.

- *My partner never seems to enjoy sex.* Talk about this in a gentle way. Encourage your partner to discover their own sexual feelings. Then start getting to know your partner's body as if for the first time. Start by massaging each other in a non-sexual way. Relax together in bed. Let your partner dictate the pace. Stay patient. Once your partner feels relaxed and comfortable, they will indicate to you that you can progress things further. Remember, if your partner learns to enjoy sex, you will get much greater pleasure from it too.

- *We have never had good sex together.* Again, talk about it. Allow time for each of you to say how you would like your sex life to be. How often would each of you like to make love? Take the pressure off yourselves for a while. Put sexual intercourse off the agenda. Aim to get to know and feel comfortable with one another's bodies first. Massage, touch, kiss and cuddle. See how much fun you can have in bed without having full sex. Only when you feel fully relaxed with one another should you progress to having sexual intercourse.

- *My husband is constantly demanding sex.* This is not an uncommon complaint from women. Why not make this the subject of a listening exercise? See Step Four. Listen attentively to your husband while he talks. Then repeat back what you have heard him say. Are his constant demands due to constant rejection? When you do have sex, does your husband feel pressurised to get it over with? How does that make him feel? Do you use sex as a reward or a bargaining tool?

- *My wife is never in the mood for sex.* This is also a common complaint. It often comes from the husband who is perceived as constantly demanding sex. Again, do the listening exercise. How much does your wife enjoy having sex? Has your lovemaking taken on a predictable pattern? Do you spend enough time pleasuring your wife? Do you know if and when she has an orgasm? What would your wife like to happen when you are making love? Agree to be affectionate without it having to end in sexual intercourse. Focus more on caressing and arousal. Take things slowly. Learn how to pleasure each other without any pressure. Remember, lovemaking does not always have to end in intercourse.

Reactivating Desire

No matter how diminished your sex life has become, it is always possible to get things going again. Sexual desire is like any other appetite. If it is neglected or ignored it diminishes. But a loving and supportive partner can help you rekindle the spark that had faded. Try following the steps outlined here. They are simple and practical but most effective.

- *Stay intimate* – kissing, cuddling, touching. Don't ban everything because of fear of sexual intimacy. Express love to one another around the house: children need to see their parents being playful and loving together. You are their role models for adult relationships.

- *Keep your bedroom private at certain times.* It is good for children to respect their parents' right to privacy.
- *Go to bed earlier.* That way you won't be too tired.
- *Go to bed together.* If one of you wants a relaxing bath first, that's fine.
- *Make your bedroom an IT-free zone.* This can work wonders.
- *Take your time.* Avoid pressure or urgency. It may take several sessions before you feel truly relaxed with one another.
- *Stay romantic.* Pay compliments. If your partner praises you, listen and accept it graciously. Compliments indicate a greater awareness of each other.
- *Don't be afraid to ask for directions.* Making love is an art and a voyage of discovery. Feedback helps a lot. Use not only words but actions too.
- *Remember that sex can improve with age.* It just requires more gentleness and time.
- *Do the intimacy exercise outlined below.* It will help you become more in touch with one another.

INTIMACY EXERCISE

Even if you enjoy a good sex life, this exercise is worth doing from time to time. It allows you to relax together, have fun and reconnect without having intercourse. Based on a programme originally designed by Masters and Johnson, this exercise helps stimulate sensory awareness. Because intercourse is excluded, a reluctant sexual partner will feel more relaxed and ready to engage in intimacy.

1. Set time aside for this exercise – preferably when you are not too tired and are both feeling relaxed. Early evenings often work well.
2. Agree in advance that there will be no sexual intercourse. This takes away fear if one partner is

resistant. It also removes the pressure of performance anxiety.

3. The wife has a long relaxing bath. Use scented oils, candles and plenty of hot water.
4. Meanwhile, the husband sets up the bedroom. Make it tidy and warm; light some candles or turn the lights down low. If you want background music, make sure that it is soft and relaxing.
5. The wife dries herself in front of a mirror while the husband bathes.
6. The wife lies on her tummy on the bed while the husband dries off.
7. The husband massages his wife's back for 8–10 minutes. Body oil or lotion is optional. No chatting. Focus on the sensation of touching and being touched.
8. Reverse roles and positions. The wife rubs her husband's back for 8–10 minutes. Stay in the moment; focus on touch.
9. The wife lies on her back. Feeling exposed or vulnerable? Respect that in each other. The husband touches the front of his wife's body, avoiding the breasts and genital area.
10. Reverse roles and positions. Again, no genital touching. Just enjoy the intimacy.

Resist the temptation to proceed to sexual intercourse. This exercise serves to reawaken and then heighten sexual excitement. It recreates the thrill you felt in the early days of your courtship, when you were getting to know each other's bodies for the first time.

ONGOING EXERCISE

As you are no doubt aware, the sexual side of your relationship is multi-faceted. What issues discussed here resonated most with you? How about your partner? It takes time and energy to bring about change. But change for the better is always worthwhile. Choose the changes that you would like to make. Try to integrate them gradually into your sex life.

Now that you have completed Step Eight, do you find it easier to talk to your partner about sex? The challenge now is to keep this topic on the agenda until you both feel totally comfortable with it.

If you have children, your newfound ease in talking about our sexual selves will be an invaluable aid to giving them a healthy attitude to their own sexuality.

Keep on enjoying sex for as long as you can. It is the most precious and special gift that you can share with your life partner.

Step Nine

TIME APART – KEEPING YOUR OWN IDENTITY

One of the most satisfying elements in the dynamic between a couple is the coming together again at the end of a day or after some time apart. Each of you has been involved in separate activities. Whether things have gone well and you are tired but happy, or you are feeling frustrated, even angry, you can now face each other and share your experiences.

When you commit to a long-term relationship, you enter a partnership. You and your partner form a team, a unit. If you have children your unit becomes a family. By nature we instinctively yearn to belong to a group, a tribe, a country, a society. It feels good to be part of a greater whole.

But there are times when your individuality can get swamped. You can become so much a part of this unit that you lose sight of the essential you. You may find at times that you are introduced to others as the partner/wife/husband of your spouse or as the mother/father of your child. You may be so busy being a partner and parent that you forget the person who was so full of ambition and enthusiasm when you were single. Perhaps your focus is now on everyone else in your family. It is good to note that in relationships that work well both parties have their own autonomy.

When You No Longer Count

If you constantly put the needs of others before your own, you may have slipped into one or more of the following patterns:

- You feel that you are losing sight of your own identity. It has become submerged by the demands of those around you. When you look at a photo of your younger self you can no longer identify with that former carefree you.
- You may start to lose confidence in your ability to act independently. You are, of course, part of a team and good team players consult with their mates on important matters. But if you have developed a pattern of seeking the endorsement of your partner for even minor decisions, perhaps your autonomy is being eroded.
- You may even find that you no longer think independently from your partner. So you constantly defer to them before forming your own opinion. When you are out socially, do you take a back seat while your partner speaks on your behalf? This is a real danger sign, so watch out for it.
- Perhaps you have also stopped keeping yourself informed of what is going on in the world outside your little unit. This ostrich approach means that your circle of interest is diminishing. Is your mind so filled with the minutiae of day-to-day living that you no longer make time to keep up with the news? Remember that ever-decreasing circles end in stagnation.
- Your interests and hobbies, which once meant so much to you, have become largely forgotten. It may be that you no longer have the same interests. But have you developed other interests for yourself? To do so requires time and you may not have made that time for yourself.
- You are not sure of yourself any more. Your ego has wilted from lack of attention. If others pay you a compliment you dismiss the message, telling yourself that they don't really mean it; they are just trying to be kind.
- You may wonder sometimes if you are becoming depressed. For as your world diminishes, so too does your self-image.
- You begin to feel badly about yourself, then to dislike yourself. Some people describe this stage as feeling heavy, dull, weighed down. A mantra of '*I'm so hopeless*' has lodged itself inside your head.

- You may start avoiding situations where you will stand out, where you fear you will be noticed.
- As you lose contact with the person who is you, you may take less care about your appearance. You spend money on clothes for others in your family, but not on yourself.
- You lose sight of your own needs. *'Any old thing will do for me because I don't matter'* is the message in your head.
- If you see yourself in a mirror it is only by accident.

If any of these scenarios ring true for you, it is time to take action. Remember that if you are feeling low, the knock-on effects impact negatively not only on yourself but on your partner and family.

Together Forever

If couples are unemployed or both work from home, finding time apart can be a challenge. For some couples this togetherness can develop into co-dependency. Each must know where the other is and precisely what they are doing whenever they are apart. In extreme cases, one partner takes on the role of director while the other adapts to being constantly questioned and held accountable.

So if you work together, be sure to spend some of your downtime apart. Insist on making this time for yourself. Look on it as a survival imperative, not just for you but for your relationship with your partner.

Develop an interest, something that you really enjoy. Think back to the person you were before you met your partner. What were your ambitions and interests? What would you like to take up again?

Case Study

Meet Robin and Dara. They have been in a relationship for three years and got married last year. They share many interests: walking, eating out, theatre and the same sense of humour. They have a good social life with many friends.

Look Out for Your Partner

Once you have taken care of yourself, make sure that your partner has time off to do the same. Outside contact stimulates us all. You and your partner will benefit from being introduced to new people, new perspectives and new outlooks.

You will also find that having some time apart for yourselves makes your relationship stronger. A temporary escape from each other and from the weight of responsibility will give each of you a new perspective on your lives. And it is good to feel that you respect each other's individuality and different interests.

SESSION ONE

Answer the following questions in your notebook:

1. Do you feel that you have lost your identity or autonomy somewhat since getting married or moving in with your partner?
2. Are you happy with the amount of free time you have at the moment?
3. How do you feel about the amount of time your partner spends away from you?
4. Name three activities you like to do without your partner.
5. Name three activities your partner likes to do without you.
6. If you were to spend more time away from your partner/children, how would you feel?
7. Would you like your partner to take more time out alone or with friends?
8. What are your feelings about spending time away from your partner?
9. Can you name any of your needs that are not being met in your relationship?
10. When did you last take time off for yourself?

Now share your answers with your partner; talk about what you would both like to change. Then agree on taking individual time out.

SESSION TWO

Organising Your Own Downtime

If you have a busy lifestyle, your time apart is precious. You will want to use it wisely. Read over your notes from Step One. Which of your unfulfilled ambitions can you address now? Set yourself goals here, making sure that they are reasonable and achievable.

Choose one three-hour slot per week as your time for yourself. What interests would you like to develop? Is it to keep fit or to take up a hobby? What classes are available locally? Do you know of any friends who may wish to do this activity with you? If money is an issue you can always go for a speed walk or jog with or without friends. If you are musical, is there a local choir you could join? Check out classes in your local community college – they are never too expensive.

Some Tips

- Choose an activity that you enjoy – this is not a time for making yourself do something that you feel you ought to do.
- Take stock after a few weeks. Are you enjoying your time apart? How do you feel when you get home afterwards? The aim is to make you feel good about yourself – invigorated, stimulated, happy.
- If you are not happy with what you have chosen to do, change it. Do not feel compelled to persevere in a course that you are not enjoying.
- However, do allow yourself time to settle into whatever activity you have chosen. Don't dismiss it out of hand too soon.

- Avoid bringing more stress onto yourself. Do not undertake a course that culminates in a final exam unless that is something you really want to do.
- Do not worry if your partner is not interested in your activity. Remember, this is a time for you to do what you want to do.
- If your partner is interested, give an account of what you enjoy about your time out.
- Encourage your partner to take advantage of their time out. This helps keep the balance in the relationship.
- Avoid the expense of babysitters by each partner covering for the other.

ONGOING EXERCISE

Stick to your time-out commitment. You are not being selfish by undertaking an activity for yourself. This feeling of guilt is particularly common when you have children. Believe me, you will be a much happier and better partner and parent once you have had a little time to yourself. Log your experience in your notebook. Record how you feel each week.

- Is your time apart helping you to view the smaller irritations of your life with more detachment?
- Is your level of self-confidence improving?
- Do you feel more in touch with the essential/inner you?
- What do you most enjoy about your time apart?
- Is your partner enjoying their time apart?
- Have you become more efficient at organising your time in general?
- Have you achieved a better work–play balance in your life?
- Are you a happier person these days?

Note

It requires generosity to allow your partner some time off. If you feel resentment, try to articulate why. Maybe you feel that your partner already has sufficient time away from home while you are more tied down. But by allowing each other some relaxing time apart you show that you care about your partner as a person in their own right.

This step of the programme is particularly important for couples who spend a lot of time together – those who work together, those who are constantly in touch with one another or retired couples. Sometimes couples who spend too much time together can develop an over-dependence on each other. One partner insists on knowing where the other one is at all times.

This lack of space can lead to a form of emotional suffocation – the overwhelmed partner eventually feels incapable of independent action or thought. So, if this scenario sounds even vaguely familiar, start planning your time apart right away. You need it for your own health and the future of your relationship.

If you are concerned that your partner is going to have too much time off, don't worry. In Step Ten we will look at how you function as partners in this relationship. We will examine the balance of duties and responsibilities. But for now, get going with your time apart and trust that soon you will both be feeling happier.

Step Ten

SHARING THE WORKLOAD – PARTNERS AT HOME

On the day that you and your spouse committed to sharing your relationship in marriage, to living together, you undertook to rearrange your lives. Single life has many advantages – your freedom to come and go, to choose when and what to eat, an absolute say in which TV programme to watch. But that was then. Now you have found someone with whom you wish to share your life – someone to love in a very special way, someone who loves you too. So your life cannot be the same as it used to be. Cohabitation requires quite a bit of adjustment.

In this final stage of *Rekindle the Spark*, the challenge is for each of you to assess yourselves and each other as partners. It is good to stop every now and then and look at your contribution to the running of your lives together. The seesaw image returns.

Here in Step Ten you are asked to consider if you and your spouse have a balanced partnership and to find out how your partner feels about the roles each of you play. If you are the chief earner, you may feel justified in contributing less time to the running of the house when you are at home. If so, you are now going to find out how your partner feels about this.

Sometimes couples negotiate an arrangement whereby tasks are allocated quite specifically. If this suits, do it. But more often each partner gravitates to certain tasks so that the division comes about naturally. However, if you feel resentment in the air, either yours or your partner's, talk about it.

When you committed to sharing your lives together you probably spent very little time discussing how you would share the duties and responsibilities of running your home and your lives. There was so much else to focus on. But as time goes by the workload evolves. You gravitate towards the tasks with which you are most familiar or comfortable. This often reflects your own family background. Perhaps you see certain tasks as gender-related: women do the housework, men do the gardening. But what about your partner? Maybe in their family, tasks were not allocated so specifically. Holding on too rigidly to preconceptions from your past can lead to confusion or even conflict in the relationship.

The Martyr Syndrome

With certain couples the allocation of tasks is never properly addressed. This is sometimes because one partner opts to take on the full workload. Read the case study below. Does any of it resonate with you?

Case Study

Let's look at the story of Tanya and Len. Despite the fact that they both work outside the home, Tanya has the evening meal cooked and the house tidy by the time Len gets in from work each day.

When children come along there is little change in Len's routine. He may drop the baby to the crèche on his way to work, but all is under control when he comes home in the evening. The baby is in bed, the meal ready and the toys all put away. If he is kept late at work it is no problem. Tanya is almost relieved as that gives her more time to get everything in order.

But as time goes by, two things happen. Firstly, Len, who used to offer to help around the house, has now adjusted to this arrangement. He can even play golf at the weekend without having to feel guilty at leaving his wife to do the weekend chores. Tanya seems quite happy to do them. Besides, on the few occasions that he has tried to help out, his wife has found fault with his work.

'*He hasn't a clue*', she tells her friends happily. '*He doesn't even know where the vacuum cleaner is kept.*'

Now that he has become totally deskilled, Len sits back further in his armchair and smiles. However, a second process has also started. A niggling resentment has started to build up in Tanya. She still does everything around the house, but it really annoys her if Len puts his feet on the coffee table when she comes in to vacuum the room. Last week he even asked her to come back later – he was watching a match. He never notices the work she does. She feels he takes her for granted. Eventually, Len senses that Tanya is tense. She is mopping the floor and sighing audibly. Len offers to take over. Tanya refuses.

'*Don't be silly*', she fumes. '*You know you can't do anything right around the house. I'll just end up having to do it again after you.*'

She sighs once more as she plunges the mop back into the bucket.

Tanya has chosen to be a martyr. She enjoys the martyr role. Her favourite topic of conversation with her friends is the hopelessness and indeed laziness of men. This imbalance in their workload has a knock-on effect on the relationship between Tanya and Len. Len becomes increasingly disconnected from the running of the home. He also feels increasingly disconnected from Tanya. They have less to talk about now. Tanya is the martyr, mother and wife.

She now speaks to Len as if he were one of the children. Len, in turn, behaves more and more like a child. He sneaks in a visit to the pub on his way home from work and relishes not being caught out by Tanya. The respect they had for one another has diminished. They are no longer equal partners in this relationship.

The Innocence of Ignorance

Sometimes one partner in a relationship chooses to overlook or ignore the work that goes into keeping the home functioning. Tasks such as shopping or cooking can be considered trivial, not at all as important as work outside the home. The main earner may fall into this way of thinking.

But it is vital for a healthy relationship that all contributions are valued. If the principal earner is busy with work outside the home, they must be sure to acknowledge and show appreciation for the work that goes into the day-to-day running of the house.

Review your attitude to sharing the workload. Is there a hierarchy in how you view the tasks and responsibilities involved in running your lives together, an unspoken feeling that your contribution is somehow more important? Spend time focusing on what your partner does and how much time they spend in ensuring that your lives run smoothly.

While housework is physical, tedious and repetitive, it is also important to consider the mental or emotional workload involved in running a home. Who remembers the dates of birthdays and anniversaries; who organises cards and gifts; who plans menus for the week and arranges for the plumber to call?

Sharing in the rearing of your children is perhaps the greatest privilege of all. Many will argue that there is nothing more demanding and tiring, but ultimately satisfying and joyful, as being actively involved in the life of your child. Are you satisfied with the amount of time you spend with your child or children? What are your favourite childhood memories of time spent with one or other of your parents? What will your child's memories be?

So if you feel that you have been ignoring the demands and joys of being an equal partner in your relationship, now is the time to change.

SESSION ONE

Getting the Balance Right

Arrange a quiet time alone with notebook in hand. Write a response to each of the following questions:

1. How do you rank yourself overall as a partner in this relationship?
2. Do you think you make a fair contribution to the organisation of your home life?
3. How much do you contribute to the housework?
4. How do you score as a financial provider?
5. How well do you score yourself as a communicator?
6. If you have children, how do you contribute to the issue of child-rearing?
7. Do you think that the children feel that you, their parents, work as a team?
8. Do you have clearly defined areas of responsibility regarding home management?
9. Do you feel that the distribution of responsibility is fair?
10. If there was little or no food in the house what action would you take?
11. How would you rate yourself for this?
12. If you were starting off all over again in this relationship would you organise things differently?
13. If life at home is not going well are you inclined to blame your partner?
14. How could you handle the situation differently?
15. Are there issues regarding sharing of responsibility that cause you concern?
16. Have you discussed these with your partner?

SESSION TWO

Becoming a More Effective Team

This is a joint session with your partner.

Part A

Arrange a quiet time, free from distraction. If each of you has done Session One, go through your responses to each question. If only you have answered the questions, go through them with your partner, seeking their response and comparing them with yours.

Part B

- How do your responses compare?
- Does each of you have a different perception of your roles as partners?
- Highlight firstly the areas on which you both agree.
- Then address some of the areas of disagreement. Remember all your techniques for effective communication. If you find that you are feeling stressed or angry over an issue, suggest deferring that topic until your next session.
- In the meantime, try to put the matter into perspective. Think of a practical and fair solution. Then come back to the table. You should find that this time the issue is resolved more amicably.
- Focus on how you would like things to be – be specific; avoid generalisations or harsh criticisms.
- Play to your strengths – doing chores you like makes life much easier for you both.
- When a new distribution of tasks and responsibility is called for, agree to re-assess the situation after a given time.
- Role-play exchange – now here's a challenge. Agree to swap roles for a while. See what it is like to pay

the bills or do all the cooking for a week. Spending some time in your partner's shoes will give you a new appreciation of how they contribute to the running of your home.

- Keep it light. Admit to getting things wrong from time to time. Try to avoid taking this or any other issue too seriously. After all, you are both on the same team – right?

Revitalising Tips

Try using some of the suggestions below:

- *Relax together* – at home or by going out. Recent research tells us that couples who watch movies together report feeling closer to one another.
- *Learn together* – how about taking a course in something that interests you both: ballroom dancing, computer studies, gardening? Think about it.
- *Socialise with friends* – we all benefit from social activity. If you have very busy lives it is still good to make time to relax with friends. You can always go out together but that can be expensive. Try entertaining at home. Don't feel pressurised to produce a Michelin star meal – your friends will really appreciate a warm welcome and a simple menu.
- *Joint activities* – be they outdoor exercise or DIY at home, it is good to share in keeping fit or working. Going out at weekends as a family can be fun – fresh air and exercise have a feel-good effect on everyone. And you are helping to build up a bank of happy childhood memories for your children.
- *Keep on being romantic* – very often, actions need to come before feelings. So don't wait for a wave of romantic feeling to wash over you. Of course it is wonderful to experience that sudden rush of happiness. But it is also true that by

making a romantic gesture you will recreate that feeling of being in love all over again.

- *Little acts of kindness* – a small and random kind gesture can have a positive and powerful impact on the dynamic between you. It may not always be acknowledged, but that is not the point. It has contributed to making life that little bit easier for your partner and you will feel better for being kind.

- *'I love it when you ...'* – by recalling little actions that have made you feel special or excited, you are helping your partner to get to know you better. Saying something like, *'I love it when you call me unexpectedly – it's just the sound of your voice'* makes your spouse feel valued and special too.

- *Be appreciative* – once again, this is so simple, but sometimes overlooked. A simple *'Thank you'* to your partner can make a big difference to the dynamic between you. Taking things for granted is a habit we can slip into very easily. Try to be more conscious of the little actions or gestures that contribute to making your life richer.

Just Before You Go

Where there is life there is change. As humans we continue to develop and evolve. So do our relationships. There will always be challenges ahead. But now you are equipped with the techniques and skills to deal with them. Remember that each new skill requires practice if it is to become an integral part of the dynamic of your communication. We are all creatures of habit, so bringing about a change in attitude or behaviour takes time and patience. But know that you can make whatever changes are necessary. It just requires that you make that decision.

Conclusion

You have now completed the *Rekindle the Spark* programme. Well done!

Remember to *keep your notebooks* – your newly acquired techniques will need to be revisited before they become automatic for you both. It may also be useful to look back at your responses to some of the questions. Would you answer any of them differently today? Aren't you proud of all the insights you have gained into yourself and your partner?

Now that you can communicate better with your spouse you will find that you can use the same techniques when dealing with others. Try really listening to work colleagues, to your children, to friends and see the difference it makes. Acknowledge the other perspective when negotiating with others – they will be more likely to compromise once they feel understood.

Remember, above all, that respect is the most important ingredient in any successful relationship. If you feel that someone is lacking in respect towards you, the best way to respond is by being respectfully assertive, never aggressive.

Keep in touch with the website www.relationshipsandlove.org. Follow the blogs.

In order to help me help others with their relationship problems, I would be most grateful if you would complete the feedback form on our website.

Many thanks, keep on smiling and every good wish for you both in the future.

Barbara Duff

BIBLIOGRAPHY

Bowlby, John (1982) *Attachment: Attachment and Loss Volume One*, New York, NY: Basic Books.

Bowlby, John (1988) *A Secure Base: Parent–Child Attachment and Healthy Human Development*, London: Routledge; New York, NY: Basic Books.

British Association of Anger Management (BAAM) (2008) 'Mental Health Organisation: Boiling Point Report 2008', www.angermanage.co.uk/anger-statistics, last accessed 16 August 2017.

Chopra, Deepak (2014) 'The Secret of Attraction: Meditation' [video], *YouTube*, 7 March, www.youtube.com/watch?v=z4SoaH_pu-Y, last accessed 22 June 2017.

Debrot, Anik; Meuwly, Nathalie; Muise, Amy; Impett, Emily A.; and Schoebi, Dominik (2017) 'More Than Just Sex: Affection Mediates the Association between Sexual Activity and Well-Being', *Personality and Social Psychology Bulletin*, Vol. 43, No. 3, pp. 287–299.

Eisenberger, Naomi I. (2011) 'Why Rejection Hurts' in Max Brockman (ed.), *Future Science: Essays from the Cutting Edge*, pp. 170–183, New York, NY: Vintage Original.

Eisenberger, Naomi I.; Lieberman, Matthew D.; and Williams, Kipling D. (2003) 'Does Rejection Hurt? An fMRI Study of Social Exclusion', *Science*, Vol. 302, No. 5643, pp. 290–292.

Gottman, John M. (1994) *Why Marriages Succeed or Fail: And How You Can Make Yours Last*, New York, NY: Simon & Schuster.

Gottman, John M. and Silver, Nan (1999)*The Seven Principles for Making Marriage Work*, New York, NY: Three Rivers Press.

Huffington Post (2013) 'Poor Communication Is The #1 Reason Couples Split Up: Survey', *Huffington Post*, 20 November, www.huffingtonpost.com/2013/11/20/divorce-causes-_n_4304466.html, last accessed 22 June 2017.

Johnson, Susan (2008) *Hold Me Tight: Seven Conversations for a Lifetime of Love*, New York, NY: Little, Brown and Co.

Bibliography

Masters, William H. and Johnson, Virginia E. (1966) *Human Sexual Response*, Boston, MA: Little, Brown and Co.

Moberg, Kerstin Uvnas (2003) *The Oxytocin Factor: Tapping the Hormone of Calm, Love, and Healing*, Cambridge, MA: Da Capo Press.

Nowak, Andrzej; Vallacher, Robin R.; and Burnstein, Eugene (1998) 'Computational Social Psychology: A Neural Network Approach to Interpersonal Dynamics', in Wim B.G. Liebrand, Andrzej Nowak and Rainer Hegselmann (eds), *Computer Modeling of Social Processes*, London: Sage Publications.

Orgill, Margaret-Anne (2017) 'Poor Communication Main Cause of Marriage, Cohabitation Breakdown', *UCL News*, www.ucl.ac.uk/news/news-articles/0317/240317-poor-communication-main-cause-relationship-breakdown, last accessed 13 June 2017.

Pratt, Kim (2014) 'Psychology Tools: What Is Anger? A Secondary Emotion', *HealthyPsych*, 3 February, https://healthypsych.com/psychology-tools-what-is-anger-a-secondary-emotion, last accessed 26 June 2017.

Richardson, Celai and Halliwell, Ed (2008) 'Boiling Point: Problem Anger and What We Can Do About It', *Mental Health Foundation*, www.mentalhealth.org.uk/sites/default/files/boilingpoint.pdf, last accessed 26 June 2017.

Thích Nhất Hạnh (2008) *The Miracle of Mindfulness: The Classic Guide to Meditation by the World's Most Revered Master*, London: Rider Books.

Thích Nhất Hạnh (2017) *The Art of Living*, London: Rider Books.

Verrinder, Frances (2012) 'Stuck on You', *California Magazine*, Summer 2012 North South, https://alumni.berkeley.edu/california-magazine/summer-2012-north-south/stuck-you, last accessed 16 August 2017.

Wood, Dustin; Harms, Peter; and Vazire, Simine (2010) 'Perceiver Effects as Projective Tests: What Your Perceptions of Others Say about You', *Journal of Personality and Social Psychology*, Vol 99, No. 1, pp.174–190.

Helpful Links/Associations

Accord Ireland (Marriage and Relationship Counselling): http://accord.ie
Phone: 01 5053112   Email: info@accord.ie

Addiction Counselors Ireland: http://addictioncounsellors.ie
Phone: 01 7979187   Email: info@addictioncounsellors.ie

Al-Anon and Alateen Ireland: http://al-anon-ireland.org
Phone: 01 8732699   Email: info@alanon.ie

Alcoholics Anonymous: http://alcoholicsanonymous.ie
Phone: 01 8420700   Email: gso@alcoholicsanonymous.ie

Alcohol Programmes: http://askaboutalcohol.ie, http://coolmine.ie, http://alifewise.ie

Cognitive Behavioural Therapy: http://cbti.ie
Phone: 089 4468753   Email: info@cbti.ie

HSE (Health Service Executive): http://hse.ie/eng/health/az/C/Counselling/
Phone: 1850 24 1850   Email: hselive@hse.ie

Irish Association for Counselling and Psychotherapy: http://iacp.ie
Phone: 01 2303536   Email: iacp@iacp.ie

Irish Council for Psychotherapy: http://psychotherapycouncil.ie
Phone: 01 9058698   Email: hello@psychotherapycouncil.ie

NAPCP (National Association for Pastoral Counselling and Psychotherapy): http://www.napcp.ie
Phone: 01 8040137   Email: info@napcp.ie

Helpful Links/Associations

Psychological Society of Ireland: http://www.psihq.ie
Phone: 01 4720105   Email: info@psihq.ie

Samaritans in Ireland: http://samaritans.org/your-community
Phone: 116123   Email: jo@samaritans.org